Social Workers:

Finding Real Solutions for Real Problems

Edited by the Helen Rehr Center for Social Work Practice

The Helen Rehr Center for Social Work Practice
392 Central Park West #18P
New York, NY 10025

Cover design by Joe Caroff

IN MEMORIAM: ALMA T. YOUNG, Ed.D., LMSW

Dr. Young (1930-2012) was a social work practitioner, administrator, and educator. According to many memoirs written about her, she retired as Director of Education and Quality Assurance in the Department of Social Work Services at Mt. Sinai Medical Center after many years of service. However, she continued to maintain a faculty position as Assistant Clinical Professor in the Department of Communication and Preventive Medicine at Mt. Sinai School of Medicine.

Dr. Young had a long history of participation in leadership roles in professional and nonprofit boards and organizations providing services to children, adolescents, and families as well as those involved in education, health, and public service. Among these organizations were the American Public Health Association, the Council on Social Work Education and the National Association of Social Work. She was an active member of the Pioneers, a professional organization of social workers with more than 25 years of practice.

She also served on the board of the Helen Rehr Center for Social Work Practice, New Alternative for Children (as a founding member) and the Mt. Sinai Adolescent Health Center.

Dr. Young's contribution to social work included many seminars and workshops on a variety of issues related to the profession. Her presentations and publications reflect the diversity of her involvement in practice, health and human services, and public policy. All of which can be found in professional journals, books and monograms. One of her major contributions was in the area of quality assurance of delivered social services, particularly in the development and implementation of a structured method for documentation of social work notes to the medical chart. She held adjunct positions at Hunter College (now the

Silberman School of Social Work), the Columbia School of Social Work, and the New York University Silver School of Social Work.

Above all she continued to be dedicated to the profession of social work and its service to the public. Her colleagues remember her as a warm, knowledgeable, creative contributor in her many roles and endeavors. She will be remembered for her sense of humor, her warmth and hard work as a team member. She continues to be sorely missed as one of the original committee members in producing this book. Among her many awards for her contributions to the field, was as Social Worker of the Year for Outstanding Achievement and for Exemplary Service to the Profession.

CONTENTS

Preface   13

Lynn Ohrenstein, DSW, LCSW

Acknowledgments   15

Introduction: A Guide to the Utilization of Professional

Social Work Services   17

Barbara Silverstone, PhD, LCSW

**PART I: CLINICAL SOCIAL WORK WITH
PERSONAL AND RELATIONSHIP PROBLEMS**

Chapter 1   27

Clinical Social Work with Children and Adolescents

Florence Lieberman, DSW, LCSW

Chapter 2   43

Clinical Social Work after a Traumatic Event

Lynn Ohrenstein, DSW, LCSW

Chapter 3   57

Clinical Social Work with Adults with Anxiety
or Depression

Florence Lieberman, DSW, LCSW

Chapter 4   69

Clinical Social Work with Troubled Couples

Susan Matorin, LCSW, ACSW

Chapter 5   81

Clinical Social Work with LGBT Couples

Israel Martinez, LCSW

Chapter 6   95

Clinical Social Workers in Private Practice

Phyllis Caroff, PhD, LCSW and Patsy Turrini, LCSW

PART II: SPECIALIZED AREAS OF PRACTICE

Chapter 7   111

Social Work in the Treatment of Addiction

Janet Lerner, PhD, LCSW

Chapter 8   127

Social Work with Individuals and Families Affected by

Alzheimer's Disease or a Related Dementia

Matt Kudish, LMSW

Chapter 9   147

Social Work with Disabled Adults and Their Caregivers

Frances Brennan, LCSW

Chapter 10   163

Social Work in the Terminal Phase of Illness and

Hospice Care

Elizabeth Alvarado, LCSW, ACHP-SW

Chapter 11   181

Social Workers who are Care Managers

Leonie Nowitz, LCSW, B.C.D.

Chapter 12   195

Social Work Services in Long-Term Care

Frances Brennan, LCSW

Chapter 13   209

Social Work in a Hospital Emergency Room

Carole Friedler, LCSW

Chapter 14   223

Social Work with Hospital Patients

Alma Young, Ed.D, LMSW

Chapter 15   235

Social Work in Community Agencies and Schools

Alma Young, Ed.D, LCSW

Chapter 16   247

Social Work with Homeless Families and Individuals

John Bainbridge, BA and Susan Nayowith, PhD, ACSW

Chapter 17   259

Social Work in Legal Services Agencies

Laurel W. Eisner, JD, MSW

Chapter 18   271

A Social Worker Can Help You Find the Services
You Need

Penny Schwartz, DSW, LCSW

Conclusion: Finding Real Solutions   275

PREFACE

Lynn Ohrenstein, DSW, LCSW

This book was written out of concern on the part of the Board Members of the Helen Rehr Center for Social Work Practice. They were troubled with the lack of public awareness as to what social work is, what it does, how it helps, who it helps, and how it differs from some other helping professions. This book attempts to answer these questions. In each chapter, professionals currently practicing with different types of clients (including adolescents, older adults, and couples) and in different settings (hospitals, community agencies, schools, etc.) describe their work and include case illustrations.

In recent decades there have been many changes in the education and day-to-day practice of social workers as people's needs and problems have been affected by global changes on all levels as well as the changing venues for participation in human interactions. While the book does not cover the entire field, it does offer a good picture of some of the most common areas of practice. The format makes it possible to deal with the rapid changes and to add or update chapters as necessary. It also addresses how to find resources locally.

We hope that in addition to educating the general public about social work services, this book will be useful for social work students and those who are considering entering the profession.

ACKNOWLEDGMENTS

This book is presented by the board of the Helen Rehr Center for Social Work Practice. The Helen Rehr Center for Social Work Practice is a not–for-profit organization founded in 2010. The Center is named in honor of the late Dr. Helen Rehr, a social work pioneer, and its mission is to help enhance social work practice. The Center carries out this mission through publications, educational seminars, and collaboration with other organizations. This book is its second publication (the first was *The Florence Lieberman Collection: Reflections from a Visionary Social Worker*). The book was written by a select group of experienced social workers to enhance the general public's understanding of the social work profession.

Founding Editors:
Alma Young, Ed.D.
Lynn Ohrenstein, DSW, LCSW
Frances Brennan, LCSW
Managing Editors:
Lynn Ohrenstein, DSW, LCSW
Frances Brennan, LCSW

INTRODUCTION: A GUIDE TO THE UTILIZATION OF PROFESSIONAL SOCIAL WORK SERVICES

Barbara Silverstone, PhD, LCSW

When you or a friend or family member are dealing with a personal problem such as a difficult child, marital conflict, addiction, ill health, disability, trauma, or some other personal or family crisis, a professional social worker may be able to help you. This book explains how social workers help people with a variety of complex problems in many different settings – such as mental health clinics, hospitals, community-based organizations, nursing homes, and hospice programs, among others. Social workers are professionally trained to address the myriad of personal, family, and social problems many of us face, and they have both the expertise and the experience to help you find the relief you seek. They may work with you directly to address your concerns, or may assist you in finding a related service, such as psychiatric or medical help, which will meet your specialized needs.

This book is a guide to professional social work services. It can help you decide how to get help and where to find it. It is also useful for those considering a career in social work who seek to understand the depth, the breadth, and the distinctive skills and ethical standards of social work practice.

The Distinctive Nature of Social Work Practice

The hallmark of social work practice, and what makes it unique, is its holistic approach, which takes into consideration not only individual psychology and family dynamics, but also broader cultural and socio-economic forces. Social work addresses the impact of those external forces – such as government policies, health care institutions, employers, schools and other systems that affect people's lives – and assists clients to identify, understand, and address the challenges created by them. Social work is unique in this focus on both the internal emotional barriers and the external physical, circumstantial, and institutional barriers to their clients' psychological health and well-being. Throughout the chapters in this book, you will see examples of how social workers use this broad, holistic understanding of psychology and socioeconomic forces to help clients solve thorny personal problems.

Clinical Social Workers: The Largest Providers of Mental Health Services

The most prominent and widely practiced branch of social work is direct practice with individuals and families, otherwise known as clinical social work. These professionals provide the majority of mental health services in the United States.[1] Although licensed as social workers, some may call themselves family therapists, psychotherapists, or counselors. Clinical social work overlaps to some degree with other mental health professions such as psychology, counseling, and psychiatry. Deciding on whom to turn to for help may

---

[1] Substance Abuse and Mental Health Services Administration (SAMHSA), 2012.

depend on your particular needs and the special skills offered by the practitioners of each of those professions.

Clinical social workers practice privately or in social and health care settings such as schools, hospitals, mental health clinics, home care agencies, legal services agencies and nursing homes. Whatever their specialty, social workers collaborate with other professionals in their own and related fields.

In addition to clinical practice, other branches of social work focus on social work administration, program development, community organizing, social policy analysis and development, and organizational management, planning, and leadership.

Social Work Education and Training

Most schools of social work in the United States offer professional training of social workers at the master and bachelor levels (MSWs and BSWs). The schools are usually affiliated with a college or university, but some are free standing. The social work curriculum varies by school, but by and large includes in-depth study of the literature on human growth and development, family systems theory, working with groups, the history and evolution of social work policy and practice, therapeutic social work techniques, research on effective interventions for social and personal problems, and specialized courses in a variety of fields such as child psychology, poverty, race and social injustice, addiction, domestic violence, abused or neglected children, health care, and work with the elderly. Social workers may be licensed or "certified" in every state, based on passage of specialized post-MSW tests. Licensing varies by state but is often designated as LMSW (Licensed Master Social Worker) or, with additional training, LCSW (Licensed Clinical Social Worker).[2] A significant number of social workers also seek advanced training beyond the master's level, such as intensive education and supervised practice in a range of psychotherapeutic theories and techniques -- such as trauma interventions -- or by obtaining a doctoral degree. Most social workers – and those doing mental health work and psychotherapy in

---

[2] Social work licensing is governed by regulations adopted in each state. Many insurance policies provide some degree of coverage for the services of licensed social worker. For information about insurance coverage, contact the relevant insurer or your employer's Human Resources Department.

particular -- are LCSWs and are expected and encouraged to receive supervision by an experienced clinician for several years after completing their master's degree.

What a Clinical Social Worker Offers

All social workers bring to their practice, by virtue of their training and professional ethics[3], a focus on individuals and families within the context of their social network and the cultural, economic, and physical environments that impact their lives. The social worker will collaborate with a psychiatrist if a client's situation requires prescriptions for medications (social workers do not prescribe). The social worker will also assist clients to find other medical specialists or to deal with external, institutional, or bureaucratic problems that are causing or contributing to the client's distress.

The following chapters illustrate this unique approach by describing the variety of human problems social workers address in their work: troubled children, adolescents and

---

[3] The social work code of ethics, adopted by the National Association of Social Work, can be found at http://www.socialworkers.org/pubs/code/default.asp.

their families, problematic marital and partnership relationships, individuals suffering from anxiety or trauma, adults with disabilities and their care-giving challenges, and end of life issues for the individual and the family.

Illustrating the unique approach of clinical social workers are chapters describing their work in private practice, hospitals, community agencies and long-term care settings.

The book concludes with suggestions on how to find a qualified social worker in your local community.

Barbara Silverstone, PhD, LCSW is Chair of the Helen Rehr Center for Social Work Practice and partner in SBW Partners, PLLC, a social work consulting firm. She served as President and CEO of Lighthouse International from 1984 to 2005 and President of the Gerontological Society of America in 1988. She is co-author of You and Your Aging Parent, *now in its fourth edition.*

PART I

Clinical Social Work with Personal and Relationship Problems

CHAPTER 1

CLINICAL SOCIAL WORK WITH CHILDREN AND ADOLESCENTS

Florence Lieberman, DSW, LCSW

Introduction

It is rare for either children or adolescents to overtly ask for help. For a variety of reasons, they communicate their needs through behaviors – for example, by acting out, misbehaving, or withdrawing. As a result they are typically brought to social workers for help by parents who are disturbed -- worried, angry, or both. This may be prompted by the suggestion of teachers, physicians, or concerned relatives or friends.

Parents must give permission for any professional to treat their children. As a result, parents are very much involved in the work with their children, although appropriate confidentiality is provided to protect a child's communications with the social worker. Parents also have special knowledge about their children and the problem and should be included in treatment plans. They usually have the most helpful information, including the history of the child and the family. Sometimes the problem may be a family problem, which requires the whole family to participate in treatment. Sometimes these are family struggles with illness, income, or traumas. Some children may be emotionally troubled because of tensions in the family, the parents' own emotional difficulties, or because of the child's misperception or misunderstanding of events.

Even if the children or adolescents are not responsible for these problems, they may react to such tensions within their families. Because of their immaturity, children cannot understand things in the ways that adults might. The social worker's knowledge about family dynamics and the realities of parenting, and the worker's ability to communicate with the family as a group are important. The child or adolescent are often seen alone and then in sessions with the whole family.

Working with children and adolescents requires special training and experience, including techniques for using "play therapy" with youngsters. In addition, practitioners need listening skills, imagination, and creativity to understand and communicate with children. It cannot be done by rote, which of course is true for helping adults as well. Common sense is an essential requirement of any kind of work with people, especially with children.

Case Example: Identifying the Source of an Adolescent's Symptoms

A sixteen-year-old girl was seeing a social worker after her mother died. Though sadness and some depression are understandable, she seemed overwhelmed. She stayed away from her friends, did not interact as usual with her family, and was not able to do her schoolwork. She seemed frightened. The clinical social worker was patient and played board games with her, which seemed to be helpful. After a few weeks, the girl began to cry. She was overwhelmed with guilt because she had seen that her mother's skin looked yellow. She thought that if she had told someone about this, her mother may not have died.

Feeling guilty when someone important to you dies is understandable. As a six year old, she might feel abandoned and frightened. A ten-year-old might secretly fear she caused the disaster herself in some magical way-- because of something she did. At 16 years old, she likely feels guilty about her rebellious ways with her mother, how she was angry with her. An adult might have sadness and perhaps some guilt about what was not done, or that could have been done differently. The adult would be sad that this was no longer possible. The social worker's challenge here was to ferret out the source of the girl's overwhelming sadness and help her to understand that her mother's death was not her fault.

Case Example: Finding a Common Sense Explanation for a Child's Behavior

A school board ordered that a six-year-old be sent to a special school for children with behavioral problems because he brought a weapon to school. The child had just received a special tool from his scoutmaster, a three-in-one utensil that included knife, fork, and spoon. Excited by this, he brought it to school to show his friends. The school had the right to ban knives from school and the child's parents might have explained this to him. But when the school social worker spoke to the parents and the child, she discovered that the child did not even know the utensil was considered a lethal weapon. Fortunately, in addition to measures by his parents, the community and the media were aghast at the child's punishment; one did not need a diploma to know that the child did not mean to harm anyone. Common sense kept this little one out of a special school for behavioral problems.

Case Example: Giving Practical Help to Alleviate the Source of a Child's Symptoms

Michael, an 11-year-old boy who had been an excellent student, and a likeable and good child, suddenly began to fail his classwork and not complete his homework. He was irritable with classmates and generally looked worried and exhausted. Michael's teacher brought this to the mother's attention. The mother visited the community's family agency, where the social worker saw her first. (It is customary for the parents to be seen first, since parents usually know more about what is going on with a child or family that might be important.) She looked haggard and depressed. She began to cry as she talked about Michael, who was the eldest of three children and who had always been a wonderful child. Now, Michael's mother cried, everything was topsy-turvy. Two months ago, her husband had a terrible accident, which made him unable to work and in a lot of pain. "We are reaching the end of our resources. I cannot go to work because someone has to care for him and the children."

A clinical social worker, often called the "intake worker," conducted the first interview with the family in order to make an assessment of what was needed and in what way this particular agency might be of help. It was also an opportunity for the mother to decide if this agency might be helpful.

There were no close relatives in this family, and though some friends were helpful, there was really little they could do. Michael was very responsible and as the oldest child, he was very helpful. His father was so uncomfortable at night that Michael slept in his room and would do things for him. The mother cried and explained that she was so worn out that she needed this help.

The worker made a quick diagnosis. She agreed with the mother that Michael was a responsible child and probably because of that took on too much. Though the worker would see him, to be sure that her hunch was correct, she said "first things first". The agency would evaluate the family's need, refer the family for assistance with care for the father and work with the mother and family to plan for the best ways to deal with the family's issues. One way was to take some of the responsibility away from Michael because he was too young for such things. More intensive plans would be made to help the family and plan for management. The mother cried again; this was more than she believed would ever happen

Michael was also seen. At first, he was surly and seemed angry. But, the worker explained that the whole family was under stress, that his mother needed someone to help her, and that although Michael could help, it had to be appropriate for his age. After all, she explained, if you are *successful in school, someday you will really be able to provide for your family, but now you are only eleven. Michael cried at this and spoke about how hard it was to take care of his father at night; he worried that something would happen. When he was at school he was tired and worried about how things were at home.*

In partnership with the mother, plans were made to assist the family in the way of support, income, and future planning. More than counseling was obtained for this family. Advocacy was needed. Advocacy, in this context, means cutting through red tape and working with a variety of sources to obtain economic and other necessary help. In addition, the agency continued working with the mother, to support her efforts so she would not feel alone.

There was a lot of common sense evident in this work. In addition, there was a lot of empathy and understanding. Practical help was provided in a careful, considerate way. Michael was removed from his father's bedroom. His behavior improved, and he became again the bright and good child he had been.

The Social Worker's Challenge: Assessment and Diagnosis

Making a diagnosis of any situation is a process and a summing up of all evidence. The end result will often be a label of the condition. Diagnoses have value in facilitating understanding of the situation and planning the best way to proceed. However, a label can be inadequate in fully explaining a situation, or may even be incorrect. After all, human beings make diagnoses, and human beings are fallible.

Clinical social workers stress "assessment," which is a process that can lead to a useful diagnosis about the person and the situation. The assessment also includes a bio-psychosocial review. This involves analyzing all aspects of the client's life that might illustrate the underlying problem and how the client can be helped.

Sometimes there are cultural trends in diagnoses and how certain issues are perceived. This often occurs with children and adolescents. For example, a child who acts out and is disruptive in school is often labeled with Attention Deficit Hyperactivity Disorder (ADHD). More recently, with new understandings of autism, the number of children receiving this diagnosis has swelled. Learning problems have long been discovered in schools and have led to what are called "special education" classes. However, there are a variety of problems which can impact a child's ability to learn; a sophisticated assessment may need to be done to determine how treatment should proceed. The assessment can provide guidelines that have to be suited to the particular needs of the client and the particular situation, guidance as to treatment. Sometimes labels are applied by some who are not trained in this area. This often happens in schools, where teachers have the experience and knowledge to detect problematic behavior. Their communication to parents is of vital importance, as it will be if the appropriate professional treats the child.

Case Example: A Common Sense Solution to a Complex Problem

Tom was a ten-year-old boy who had been brought to a psychiatrist at the request of his schoolteacher who felt that something was wrong. In addition to being isolated, he was unable to keep up with his class work. A psychiatrist had given Tom a diagnosis of schizoid or possibly paranoid schizophrenia because Tom showed evidence of feeling everyone was against him. A referral was made to a clinical social worker in private practice who specialized in work with children.

The worker began with Tom's parents, who were concerned about his well-being. Besides difficulty in school, he could not keep up with his siblings. His parents were highly educated and his two siblings were doing well in school and destined for college degrees and more. Tom therefore felt isolated in school and at home. In addition, he was different because he was much taller than his peers and very thin. (In maturity, he grew to be six feet seven; instead of being the gawky, skinny boy, he looked like Mr. Universe).

Tom's only friends were his chicken and his turtle. Though he came to his sessions with the clinical social worker, he had little to say. (This is not unusual, since children usually wait until they are comfortable and feel they can trust the adult. Then they speak spontaneously, because they are sure they will be listened to.) Tom had a deep interest in gardening because his mom talked about his grandfather who worked in a large botanical park. Together, the social worker and the child planted seeds in the garden. As they played, he talked about his interest in electronics. The therapist could see that he was intelligent.

After a while, Tom talked about his problems in school and his discomfort in reading, saying he would get tired and his eyes would hurt and he had to stop. This made him very unhappy. Tom wore glasses and it had been assumed that his eyes had been evaluated and cared for. Now, the social worker arranged for a visual evaluation, which revealed that his two eyes did not focus together, and his fatigue and difficulty in reading stemmed from that. Special training and a change in glasses made some difference, but it took longer for him to get over feeling different. It is not unusual for undetected physical problems to result in difficulty reading or other problems. This is why learning problems have to be specifically defined, as appropriate assistance often is available.

Here again, as in Michael's case, the social worker focused on concrete issues – Tom's eyesight – and took action herself by arranging for Tom's eyes to be examined. The result was a much simpler and far more treatable diagnosis than schizophrenia.

Culture and Ethnicity

There is no one way for families to live, or for parents to parent. There are infinite variations between and among different cultures and even within anyone culture. Clinical social workers are aware of this and try to understand these differences, and also to respect the differences between themselves and their clients. For example, a common issue within immigrant families is concern over the stance of adolescent children. Immigrant parents may not understand the culture in the United States, which tends to encourage adolescents' developmental urge to separate from parents. This often causes deep difficulties within immigrant families and may prompt parents to bring their reluctant teenagers for treatment -- to be changed.

Social workers understand the importance to the development of personal identity of one's ethnicity, family values, and family rituals. Eventually, adolescents need to learn to respect their parents' rules, even though they may not want to follow them as rigidly as their parents might want them to. On the other hand, parents need to be aware of the differences between generations and to respect the healthy drive for independence.

Case Example: Understanding through Communication

Irene, a 16-year-old girl and the child of a traditional Greek family, was brought reluctantly to the family agency. The social worker saw the girl and the parents separately. Aware of an adolescent's need for confidentiality, she would not see the parents after she had seen their daughter. She also understood that a teenager in revolt might be "revolting" to live with.

The parents complained about how Irene dressed, the company she kept, and the places she wanted to go. They felt she did not behave the way they expected a girl to act. Both parents were immigrants from Greece, coming from a small village and with little education.

Irene complained that she was not allowed to do what all her classmates did; if she followed what her parents said and dressed as they thought proper, she would be laughed at. She also complained that they put no restrictions on her brother, who was only 2 years older.

Her parents instantly said, "But he is a boy. Girls need to be different."

The social worker's task was to further communication between parents and child and to help each respect the views of the other in order to come to a reasonable agreement. This would mean each would have to give a little. The worker suggested that the treatment plan would be for the entire family to be seen together and thought it would be good to include the son. At first, the parents did not see why he should be bothered; Irene sensed that perhaps in her brother she would have an ally.

The entire family met once a week. The family spoke of what they cherished and why; the children spoke of their desire to be successful in their new situation, pointing out that life in a big and foreign city was very different from life in a small village.

The worker did little speaking. Her goal was to facilitate understanding through communication. In the long run, the goal of "give a little, gain a little" was successful with this family.

Conclusion

These case illustrations present situations in which children, adolescents and their parents require unique interventions. The interventions promote mutual respect, understanding, and the importance of learning to listen to each other's ideas, feelings and desires. These are the characteristics that underlie a clinical social worker's approach to working with children and adolescents and their families.

Dr. Florence Lieberman (1918-2011) was a Pioneer of Clinical Social Work and one of its leaders for half a century. She was Professor Emeritus at Hunter College School of Social Work for many years, was a prolific writer and the author of many books and papers and editor of two clinical social work journals. She was the first President of the Social Work Academy of the National Academies of Practice founded in 1981and was President of the International Committee on the Advancement of Private Practice (ICAPP). Dr. Lieberman maintained her private practice in New York City until her death. She was a board member of the Helen Rehr Center for Social Work Practice.

CHAPTER 2

CLINICAL SOCIAL WORK
AFTER A TRAUMATIC EVENT

Lynn Ohrenstein, DSW, LCSW

Introduction

Something terrible has happened! Have you, a family member or a friend, experienced a traumatic incident that has deeply affected you – such as a car accident, a loved one's serious illness, loss of your home or job, a man-made or natural disaster, or an act of domestic violence or rape? If you have, it may have resulted in feelings of depression, anxiety, agitation, irritability, lack of appetite, nightmares, or sleeplessness -- to mention just a few possible symptoms.

A traumatic experience is one that involves a perceived or real threat of death, serious injury, or damage to one's physical being. It inspires intense fear, helplessness, and even horror. The feelings associated with the experience can be affected by age at the time of onset, the nature of the trauma, and associated incidents of the experience itself. For example, for young children, a very scary movie experience can stimulate an intense reaction of fear. A child who has seen a movie where a character was given bad tasting food or even poison, even if done in a comic manner, may suddenly refuse to eat certain foods, be alone at night, or socialize with the friend or adult who had been at the movie with them. She may have nightmares or be generally fearful or worried.

Experiences that stimulate intense fear, helplessness, or anxiety in one person may have little effect on another. For some of us an experience may be compounded by a previous incident, which we have blocked out. In such cases a childhood incident may return in disguised form and affect our functioning as an adult, thus causing us to re-experience the trauma.

Many clinical social workers have received special training in dealing with adults or children suffering from trauma. They may be able to help you identify the source of your anxiety and then help alleviate or eliminate completely the resulting symptoms.

Case Example: Witnessing a Car Accident

Lisa is a 43-year-old woman, married with two children, who in the company of a friend witnessed two cars colliding just as they were crossing the street and had reached the other side. Two people, each one driving their own vehicle, were removed from the wreckage and taken to a nearby hospital. It was not clear if they were dead or alive. Both women witnessing this were extremely upset and decided to forego their date and return home.

Over the next few weeks, Lisa found herself unable to get the picture of the accident out of her mind. It affected her ability to focus on her job and to get to the office on time, as she could not bring herself to drive her car. She was also extremely nervous about crossing the street and walking a few blocks to the bus. Her family life was affected by this as she had difficulty getting the children to school, shopping, or being outside in an open space.

Lisa's friend, who also had been very upset by the accident, was able shortly thereafter to resume her normal activities without too much stress and was able to drive her car. Lisa compared herself to her friend and wondered why she continued to have incapacitating reactions to the experience. She finally contacted a social agency and consulted a clinical social worker there. The social worker was trained to recognize trauma and, in talking with Lisa, realized that there were deeper issues that needed to be brought to the surface. The social worker and Lisa explored the situation together, while the worker helped Lisa to relax and develop trust so she could allow herself to remember.

Gradually, in talking about her childhood, Lisa recalled that at age 5 her mother had been in a terrible train accident and had almost died. She was bedridden and recovery took a long time, but Lisa felt she was never the same again. During the time of the accident, a year-long recovery, the entire family was upset and Lisa's father and her two older sisters had to take over running the family. In further exploration, it became clear that Lisa at age 5 had been afraid that her mother would die and, at the same time, was angry that her mother was not there for her. This is not an unusual reaction for a 5-year-old. Lisa had become rebellious and was frequently punished. So just when she needed love and understanding the most, she felt the family withdrawing from her.

With the clinical social worker's understanding of the impact of such a trauma on the entire family, she helped Lisa to understand that her father and sisters were also very upset at the time by all that had happened. They may have been unable to give her the attention that she needed, but it did not mean they didn't love her. After her mother's accident, both as a child and a young woman, Lisa tried to avoid traveling as much as possible, although she did drive a car as it was necessary for her job and where she lived. When the collision happened in front of her so many years later, she once again felt vulnerable and unsafe. Restriction of movement outside seemed like the only answer. Her family, her husband and children, were annoyed with her as her reticence complicated family life. It made Lisa feel unloved and needy as she had once felt as a 5-year-old.

The social worker helped Lisa to make the connection between the trauma she experienced as a 5-year-old and her reaction at age 43 to a car accident. If this connection had not been made, the fear of cars and being in open spaces, which already curtailed her activities from her earlier trauma, would have become even more fixed with more avoidant behaviors further isolating her and interfering with her ability to integrate this experience and move forward. With the social worker's help, Lisa was gradually able to resume her normal activities and to talk to her friend about how terrible the experience had been for both of them.

Case Example: A Child's Fear

On September 11, 2001, Jake was 4 years old. He lived with his parents and his older brother Alex, age 8, in Battery Park City near the World Trade Center. The windows of Alex's room faced the North World Trade Center Tower and on 9/11, before his mother could get him out of the room, he witnessed the planes crashing into the towers. He saw the buildings burning and bodies falling or jumping out the windows.

*Alex's mother tried to deal with Alex's horror at what he
had seen and she instructed him not to say anything to
Jake. She knew that Alex had probably seen terrible things
but they never spoke about it. The family, like many others
at that time, left the city. Their apartment was not safe
because of the dangerous chemicals released into the air
from the surrounding collapsing buildings. They were away
for about eight months before returning to the city. The
mother sought social work services, as many families in the
neighborhood did at the time, because she was concerned
about the boys. During the time they lived away, in a
suburb of the city with the maternal grandparents, Alex
seemed to adjust quickly to his new school and new friends.*

*However, Jake – in contrast -- exhibited troublesome
behavior. He became generally fearful and anxious about
being outside, particularly where there were trees. He also
expressed anxiety when he heard birds chirping in the trees
or elsewhere. It reached a point when he would not play
outside with friends and only wanted to have an adult with
him. This behavior was strange to the parents as Jake had
been a friendly, outgoing, independent child. The parents
felt that it had something to do with 9/11 and a change*

from the city to the suburbs and general tensions in the city before they left, but didn't know what it could be.

Jake's parents reached out for help from a clinical social worker who was trained to work with young children. The worker understood Jake's developmental stage and knew something had happened to frighten him. Jake repeatedly played a game with items dropping from a high point to the floor. Discussing this with him, he didn't seem to connect the game with the planes flying into the buildings. Jake had not really seen anything except some destruction on the ground before they moved away. Although Alex was sure he had never said anything to Jake about what he had seen, Jake's preoccupation with things falling down was significant. After some exploration the social worker learned that Alex may have commented to a friend in Jake's presence about seeing the bodies falling out of the windows, like birds flying and falling to the ground. In the social worker's further discussion with the whole family, Jake was able to confirm this and said he had heard Alex say something about birds falling and it stayed in his mind. He was fearful that when he was outside that birds could fall to the ground and hit him and also he didn't want to see them hurt or die. In time, with many discussions about birds and their ability to fly and stay afloat and lots of positive stories regarding birds, Jake was able to once again play outside and not be as traumatized. He gradually became less fearful and could resume being a 5-year-old with his friends.

This case exemplifies the skill of the clinical social worker in understanding the symptoms of trauma and the importance of dealing with the entire family to unearth the source of a child's behavioral problems.

Case Example: A Father's Childhood Trauma and His Difficulty Finding Work

Mr. K, a 45-year-old recent refugee from Turkey living with his wife and two children, in Brooklyn, was unable to follow through on referrals from a job training and placement agency. He had been referred three times for jobs, but never pursued them and could not explain why. The agency was about to give up trying when they decided to refer the situation to a clinical social worker who was a consultant to their program.

It was not easy talking to Mr. K, as his English was minimal and he was very guarded and seemed apprehensive. The clinical social worker gradually learned that he had been a baker by trade in his home country. He loved the work and had been very grateful and happy that the placement agency had taken an interest in him. So then why did he not follow through? The social worker, who was trained in trauma work, began to suspect some underlying causes. She spent a number of interviews exploring his childhood and despite his limited English, she learned a little of his earlier history.

One detail in particular impressed her, which she further discussed with him. When he was eight years old his father had been held in a dungeon-type prison for some offense he was accused of. Mr. K. and his mother were able to visit. It was located underground and Mr. K remembered the foul smells, the dampness and his increasing inability to breathe. He often felt panicked, until one day he rebelled against visiting his father. His father died in this prison and Mr. K felt his mother never forgave him for withdrawing from the visitation. While she never accused him, he believed she blamed him for his father's death. He blamed himself as well.

Mr. K apparently had blocked out a lot of this and he was surprised that it was all coming back to him. In further conversations the clinical social worker learned that all three jobs he was referred to had one factor in common. In two he needed to go underground to get to the subway and in the third, which was a bakery located near his home – a seemingly perfect job for him -- he had to walk down two flights. The clinical social worker helped Mr. K. make the connection between his avoidance of underground, dark, damp places to this earlier experience of being frightened that he could not breathe. He also remembered his guilty feeling that he had rejected his father and that may have killed him.

Mr. K. volunteered that his whole life must have been affected in this way, since he couldn't live in or go into a basement or other places that had the damp odors he associated with his father's prison. His avoidance behaviors had caused problems in his marriage as his wife was angry and couldn't understand why he did not take advantage of the job opportunities that would have made life easier for the whole family. In spite of Mr. K.'s limited English, with the social worker's assistance, he was able to understand how the emotional connection to the childhood

trauma of his father's imprisonment and death had affected
many areas of his life. With this understanding, he became
more willing to venture out. He agreed to try the bakery job
and was able to venture underground, all the time
repeating to himself that it was not a prison or foul
smelling place.

Post-Traumatic Stress Disorder (PTSD)

Most of us exposed to traumatic stress are able to go on
with our lives even though we may be pre-occupied by the
event and have intrusive memories for a while. This is a
normal way of responding to terrible experiences. It is only
after a passage of time when we are unable to integrate the
experience that specific patterns of avoidance and
hypersensitivity to certain cues develop. If we begin to
arrange our lives around the trauma, avoiding certain
experiences, areas, and activities that remind us of the
trauma, we may be experiencing Post-Traumatic Stress
Disorder (PTSD), which is more problematic. In two of the
examples above, the cases of Lisa and Jake, help was
sought for symptoms of PTSD before the avoidant
behaviors became more fixed and separated from the

original traumatic incident. In the third example, Mr. K, his avoidance of dark and damp places had taken on a life of its own over many years. He was fortunate that the agency was able to use the services of a consultant social worker to help him, since the PTSD wasn't obvious and the man's behavior didn't make sense to anyone else.

In the case of Lisa she was able with help from the clinical social worker to connect her recent inability to resume normal life to a trauma in her childhood. If this connection had not been made, her symptoms would likely have become worse and more disruptive of her life and the functioning of her family. Similarly, if Jake had not been seen by a skilled clinician, as he was growing up he might have developed fear of planes, living in an apartment building on a high floor, or being able to work in certain locations. This would certainly have narrowed his life, limiting many opportunities and experiences. In the case of Mr. K. we could already see how this early childhood experience had limited his life and that of his family.

Conclusion

A clinical social worker trained in trauma work can help uncover the origin of certain dysfunctional behaviors that are a symptom of unresolved trauma, or PTSD. When behaviors, feelings or thoughts do not make sense to us, we become fearful and try to suppress them. This is a natural reaction. It is important to recognize the fear and get help for it. There has to be a reason and explanation that can unlock the mystery. We only need to take a chance, and overcome our fear of reaching out for help.

Lynn Ohrenstein, DSW, LCSW has been a practitioner, supervisor, and director of a mental health clinic at Jewish Board of Family& Children Services. In her many areas of practice, she worked with and served as a consultant to special populations. She also directed a training program at the Jewish Board for Russian social work students. She has focused on the impact of trauma on adults, children, and their families. Dr. Ohrenstein has maintained a private practice in New York City for many years. She is a board member of the Helen Rehr Center for Social Work Practice.

CHAPTER 3

CLINICAL SOCIAL WORK WITH ADULTS WITH ANXIETY OR DEPRESSION

Florence Lieberman, DSW, LCSW

Introduction

Are you anxious? Are you blue? Are you fearful? Many people suffer from these troubling feelings at various times in their lives. Emotions are a natural part of human experience, some pleasant and some very unpleasant. Anxiety and depression are two common upsetting emotions that many people experience from time to time, or even on a regular, chronic basis. While it is natural to try to avoid such disturbing emotions, these feelings are usually communicating a message of some sort and should not be ignored or pushed aside. A better approach would be to discuss them with the help of a clinical social worker who can help a person to identify the sources of the distress and to develop ways to reduce or eliminate it.

Social workers are trained to assist people with many life problems by seeking explanations in their personal and family histories and their current life challenges. They are skilled in addressing individuals holistically, considering the many factors and influences that affect a person's emotional state. These may include life crises, haunting memories, the relationship between current and past experiences, and even physical ailments.

Social workers understand that there is a complex relationship between the mind and the body. Emotions are felt and experienced in many cases as a physical problem, such as heart palpitations, sleeplessness, loss of appetite, or aches and pains. Since the mind is a part of the body, it is not uncommon for emotional problems to be expressed in physical ways. It is also true that some physical problems may cause psychological symptoms. The holistic approach used by social workers enables them to consider all the facets of a person's life in finding the possible causes for her or his emotional distress.

Anxiety

Anxiety is a very common feeling that most people have experienced at one time or the other. Anxiety usually means someone is afraid of something, although it may not always be clear what that is. Sometimes the fear is rational and appropriate. It may be a warning, a signal that something is dangerous and should be avoided. In this sense, anxiety is protective – a rational response to danger that can provoke the individual to deal with or avoid the danger. In most of these situations, the anxiety calls upon the body and the mind to prevent and/or deal with the problem.

There are many events that typically create rational, appropriate anxiety, for example an important examination, a job interview, a first date, or a new social situation. The degree of anxiety varies with individuals and circumstances. However, in some cases the anxiety is not related to any discernible rational danger, or is completely out of proportion to an actual danger or the likelihood the feared event will occur. For some, particular circumstances create great anxiety, so great that the person feels out of control and may be incapacitated with fear. In such cases, people may seek medication to alleviate their symptoms, or turn to alcohol or drugs or aggression to mask the emotional pain. Although these may provide temporary, short-term relief, a far stronger and more lasting remedy would be to get to the bottom of the anxiety.

Case Example: Irrational and Excessive Anxiety

Mrs. Brown sought help from a clinical social worker because she was so nervous about her daughter's pregnancy that she could not sleep and often could not eat. Since Mrs. Brown had two children, the social worker asked her how she managed her own pregnancies. "It was hell" she said. Medication was not helpful and anyway had to be avoided during her pregnancies. Her sleeping was minimal. She had bad dreams and little appetite. She was worried that the baby would have something wrong with it, and she didn't know why this worried her so. The first child was normal but Mrs. Brown was equally anxious and fearful during her second pregnancy. She worried incessantly. Although it is normal for parents to be concerned a bit during pregnancy, Mrs. Brown's anxiety was extreme and disproportionate to the likelihood of a problem occurring. Now these intense, irrational, and

excessive fears had recurred with the pregnancy of Mrs.
Brown's daughter. She had no idea why.

The social worker asked if something had happened that
might have made her so afraid. Since Mrs. Brown could not
recall anything, the social worker encouraged her to talk
about her life experiences. She explained that she was the
middle child of three. There was an older brother and a
younger sister, but she never really knew the sister. Mrs.
Brown said she was too young, less than 1 year old, when
this sister died.

Her older brother was someone everyone loved even
though he was mentally challenged. When Mrs. Brown was
15, her parents placed him in an institution. She did not
know why they did this and she missed him. The social
worker asked whether Mrs. Brown had any relatives who
might know something about what happened to her
siblings. She said there was only one aunt and the social
worker encouraged Mrs. Brown to ask her about it. Mrs.
Brown procrastinated for several weeks, as if she was
afraid to learn the truth.

Eventually Mrs. Brown learned that she was 11 years of age – not one year old -- when her sister died. Her sister had been born with multiple handicaps. Mrs. Brown cried, "I think I thought my mother had killed her."

Now, with this information brought into the light of day, the social worker and the client understood the source of Mrs. Brown's fear of having a damaged child or grandchild. It was something anyone with two siblings with serious problems would have been likely to feel, although not to the extreme degree as Mrs. Brown. Mrs. Brown's two daughters were healthy. Mrs. Brown now began to recall her mother's depression and possible envy of her sisters who had four healthy children. Mrs. Brown had felt enormous pressure as a child to do everything right, to be good and perfect – perhaps to assuage her mother's sorrow.

The social worker and Mrs. Brown talked more about her disabled brother and together they explored the possibility that Mrs. Brown's parents were afraid that her suitors would be frightened off when they met him. Mrs. Brown also cried about that fact that when her brother died, her parents had not placed a headstone on his grave.

Mourning, at long last, the loss of her siblings, and understanding how the death (of her sister) and the disappearance (of her brother) had triggered her irrational fears, helped Mrs. Brown cope over time with the birth of three more grandchildren. She was understandably tense until she saw them, but no longer pathologically anxious. Symbolically, she put a headstone on her brother's grave, thereby bringing the mourning process to an end.

The social worker's skillful guidance had led to the answers and the remedy for irrational and debilitating anxiety.

Depression

Depression is more insidious than anxiety and sometimes can be severely immobilizing. A person suffering from depression feels hopeless, that nothing will change, or that something unpleasant, bad, or dangerous has already occurred that cannot be remedied. Feeling hopeless and helpless are frightening and quite debilitating. Some people suffering from these feelings realize something is wrong and they muster their resources and fight back against the feelings of helplessness. This is a way of coping and requires a great deal of inner strength. This is how some people deal with tragedy, others with the loss of physical stamina and prowess in old age.

But there are many others who are unable to do any of this and have given up all hope. Pathological depression, which may lead to failure to eat or carry on daily activities, is often treated medically with good results. But a clinical social worker can approach it differently. With time, care and insight, depression can be understood and alleviated, perhaps with accompanying medical treatment, or in some cases without the need for it.

Case Example: Depression Caused by a Physical Problem

Mrs. Herman became very depressed, with no energy, no appetite, and an inability to carry on her usual activities. Her family brought her to see a social worker in the family agency in their community. When her social worker could find no precipitating incidents for the current depression and nothing that might reawaken old feelings, she suggested a thorough physical examination. This quickly revealed that Mrs. Herman was suffering from a serious case of diabetes. Studies show that people with diabetes have a greater risk of depression, and when it is untreated, as in Mrs. Herman's case, there is often a loss of appetite and low energy. Treatment of Mrs. Herman's illness resulted in better health and her symptoms of depression improved.

In this case, the social worker searched for both emotional and physical sources of Mrs. Herman's symptoms, and successfully facilitated the client's improved health and emotional well-being.

Case Example: Depression and a Buried Childhood Trauma

Mrs. Jennings had sought help from a social worker because she had very little energy and there was little joy in her life. She was unhappy all of the time. Worse, she felt completely helpless with no hope that things could be better.

She was married and the mother of two young children, but took no pleasure in any of this. She felt overwhelmed by *everything she was supposed to do. She said that as a child she was the least capable person in her family, which consisted of two sisters, a brother, and herself. She said she had always been weak and unable to do what everyone else did. She said, "They have always had to worry about me."*

When asked to talk about her history, her life, she indicated "it was never good" and she "never felt like she was anything." Though she had very little memory of it, her family had talked from time to time about how she had been hospitalized at age 2 with a serious back condition that made it necessary for her to lie perfectly still. She always was ill, and always had to be cared for.
Because of the age of her first hospitalization she did not remember much. She certainly could not have understood what it was all about. She said she had a vague memory or feeling of being tied down all her life. She would be hysterical if anything was too tight or too loose.

The social worker spoke with Mrs. Jennings about what such an experience might feel like for a child who was too young to really understand and what it might mean to a family that had to worry about a child like this. This took many sessions of talking and crying. Eventually Mrs.

Jennings understood the source of her chronic feelings of helplessness. She began to realize that she could no longer be tied down against her will, that she was no longer helpless and that she was no longer ill. And in the long run, Mrs. Jennings became an able and helpful member in her own family.

Conclusion

Social workers pride themselves on being able to attend to the entire gamut (called the bio-psychosocial situation) of the person seeking help. Experience has taught us that there are reasons behind conditions such as anxiety or depression that may seem to be senseless or pathological. They need only to be brought into the light of day.

Dr. Florence Lieberman (1918-2011) was a Pioneer of Clinical Social Work and one of its leaders for half a century. She was Professor Emeritus at Hunter College School of Social Work for many years, was a prolific writer and the author of many books and papers and editor of two clinical social work journals. She was the first President of the Social Work Academy of the National Academies of Practice founded in 1981and was President of the International Committee on the Advancement of Private Practice (ICAPP).Dr. Lieberman maintained her private practice in New York City until her death. She was a board member of the Helen Rehr Center for Social Work Practice.

CHAPTER 4

CLINICAL SOCIAL WORK WITH TROUBLED COUPLES

Susan Matorin, LCSW, ACSW

Introduction

Most couples are able to form a relationship built on common goals, the use of problem solving techniques, and other ways of dealing with life issues. They enjoy many benefits of a loyal trusting intimate partnership and share many interests. In time they learn to compromise, divide up daily tasks fairly, work out differing ideas regarding how much time to spend together or apart and how to manage family obligations. They preserve a romantic spark and do not allow daily pressures and tasks to drown out time for some fun. Good communication and a sense of humor provide the glue when the inevitable stress occurs. People learn how to make personal sacrifices, to not always get their own way, but for the greater good of the team.

But for some couples, their initial romantic hopes can collapse. Disagreements take on a life of their own, compromises feel humiliating, and hurts fester. A professional social worker can be very helpful when people are persistently unhappy in the relationship, chronically disappointed, or in open conflict with their partner. Making a decision to seek help and put the brakes on a deteriorating situation can be scary. In American culture, women are often more comfortable seeking help. They are often the ones that make the first call and lean on the reluctant partner to join.

How can a professional social worker help? Social workers are nonjudgmental. Expert in improving communication, they understand that people who are upset and frustrated express themselves poorly. Social workers appreciate the big picture. The clients' personality styles, life experience, and cultural and religious beliefs all affect how they handle problems. Social workers can tease out and highlight positives which people can draw on to solve their problems.

On rare occasions, a partner may have made a decision to divorce prior to counseling. Most couples, however, need reassurance that counseling can improve rather than disrupt their family. Couples will commonly inquire whether or not the social worker is married. They are not asking for personal information, just assurance that the social worker has sufficient life experience to know that relationships are a challenge!

These are some common problems that can benefit from counseling:

(1) Some families express disapproval of one's choice of partner. It can feel very hurtful and upsetting to defend one's choice and experience immediate loyalty conflicts as one forms his/her own family.

(2) Some families intrude and take over the wedding planning! This unpleasant experience forces an individual to "grow up" and learn to set a boundary to protect the new relationship.

(3) Individuals raised in a divorced home may have painful childhood memories of parents who could not work out their differences. Anxieties about trust and commitment are natural.

(4) Compromise can be tough. It is so tempting to impose on a partner one's own way of doing things. Couples are often challenged to learn how to pick and choose their battles and when to give in.

(5) With partnerships come many joint decisions: such as whether to have a child; managing the pressures of a two-career family; or finding the teamwork to parent. Couples also must face the unexpected: a job loss, a frightening illness, and caregiver demands for older parents.

(6) Couples who are empty nesters have invested time and energy to raise a family. Once that work is done, some couples have difficulty reconnecting and reclaiming their relationship without that focus. They may not share interests and may not agree on how to spend newfound time together.

(7) Additional problems can arise if one person has a very prickly personality and quickness to argue, or clings to rigid cultural or religious differences.

(8) Even if one partner has made the decision to end the relationship, a social worker can still be very helpful. When a couple breaks up it is natural for one or both partners to feel bitter, hurt, and angry and struggle with feelings of failure. A social worker can help couples deal with these

very painful feelings and learn to co parent successfully if there are children.

(9) Sex. Most social workers believe that healthy relationships of all ages include some intimacy. Sadly, many couples let this fall by the wayside. A social worker can help couples get over the awkward embarrassment to include this important topic in the discussion.

The First Meeting

This is what a couple might expect for a first appointment with a social worker:

The social worker meets first with both people together. This is the best way to establish neutrality and form an alliance with both people. The social worker allows both people to tell their story and reasons for wanting help. It is very important to establish whether this is a crisis or a longer standing problem. The social worker gathers information about the history of the relationship, childhood families, education, work, religion, and culture. The social worker may organize this information on a family tree type diagram, which visualizes for the couple their backgrounds, their networks of support, and provides a snapshot of their situation. For example, such a diagram may highlight that one individual was raised as an only child in a two career professional family; and the partner by contrast is one of four siblings with a stay-at-home mom. We might predict that differing viewpoints about the role of a woman and family size could emerge for this couple.

The social worker sets a few simple but clear rules for constructive discussion and enforces them, especially when emotions run high. These include no interrupting, no finger pointing, and no use of derogatory words. These rules are immediately helpful as they set the tone for a respectful airing of differences and allow each person to feel heard.

Couples in trouble tend to blame their partners and take themselves off the hook. To combat this, the social worker will restate a complaint into a relationship problem. "It sounds like you are overwhelmed by the demands of having a new baby and juggling your careers." It sounds like you disagree about how much time you should give to your parents." "It sounds like you are feeling pressured by him to have another child." "I have the sense time for your private relationship gets put on the back burner as you take care of everyone else." These statements help focus the counseling in jargon free language.

In this initial meeting, the social worker will acknowledge that the couple is taking a step in the right direction by coming for help. The social worker will take note of some positives ("I see you both share a value of caring for your parents") but then highlight ways each person will need to change their behavior to improve the relationship. For example: "I see how upset you are but I notice your tone is quite critical -- is that something you are aware of?"

Next the social worker will meet with each person individually. These meetings can be brief if the couple is facing a crisis. This allows each individual to share more personal information, for example about a past relationship or a current secret that can spill into the current problem.

Often couples will ask about length of time for the counseling. It is not easy to provide an immediate answer as the frequency and duration of counseling depends on how urgent and/ or serious the problem is, as well as the couple's financial resources and insurance benefits. But people expect a time frame. The social worker will assure the couple that the work will include agreed upon goals, and that he or she appreciates the financial cost of therapy. Troubled couples will often invest more easily in a costly but tangible item for their home rather than in counseling to improve the emotional climate of that home. Often when a relationship is in trouble, the couple will distract themselves by embarking on a costly renovation project -- adding to the stress and bickering over details!

Lastly, a social worker will give couples hope. However painful their problems, a social worker may assure the couple that their issues can be worked out. Without raising false expectations, the social worker will give the couple credit for taking action and pressing the pause button. This may counter the couple's overwhelming anxieties and discouragement.

Case Example: A Bickering Couple

A friend referred Karen and Charles to Ms. S. Married 5 years, they wanted a child but were concerned about their excessive bickering. They wisely believed they should do better together before adding a baby to the mix. Despite being accomplished in their careers, a simple task like renting a car for a trip could result in angry frustrated interactions, often in public.

Often the presenting concern--the issue that prompts a couple to ask for help--covers more serious problems. Karen was angry about Charles's workaholic behavior, long office hours, and how much time he spent on the computer when he was at home. She longed for more affection and down time with him. She had a playful personality. This was expressed even in her casual clothing, a funky style with Converse sneakers.

Charles had an anxious, detail-oriented personality. He had a formal, business-like manner. Karen felt nagged about her weight, a very sore subject. Charles felt angry that Karen showed no discipline about diet and exercise and had put on weight since their wedding. While Karen acknowledged the weight issue, she felt hurt and wanted to be loved for herself "not for some perfect" body. Charles was also upset about Karen's social drinking, both for the extra calories and how, in his view, it changed her behavior for the worse. About this Karen was quite defensive.

Ms. S met with them twice a month. Despite their anger and unhappiness, they were committed to do better, and their pressured careers made scheduling tough.

Karen and Charles were products of very difficult divorces. Karen experienced her mother as highly intrusive and critical, and would still have screaming phone fights with her. Charles's parents divorced when he was in college. He experienced his Dad as ineffectual in earning a living and taking care of serious health issues.

Armed with this valuable information Ms. S helped Karen recognize how she overreacted to Charles's concerns as if he was her critical mother. Ms. S set a firm limit on screaming whatever the frustrations. Charles came to better understand his desperation to avoid repeating his dad's failures. The social worker helped him retain his high standards, but to relax these harsh expectations and not impose his anxiety onto Karen.

This couple experienced relief and progress when they learned to manage everyday tasks with less bickering. Karen became pregnant and gave up alcohol. Charles admired her discipline. Karen supported Charles through a career upheaval and offered very helpful advice; he helped her set limits when her mother misfired with intrusions.

Conclusion

It is common for couples to remain in counseling to better manage life challenges or to return for a tune-up. Karen and Charles have chosen to return after their child's birth to manage their apprehensions about becoming parents while balancing demanding careers. As products of painful divorces, they have some real fears and insecurities about their capacity to be loving parents. Multiple sets of loving grandparents nonetheless also present fresh boundary issues.

Couple treatment is a unique sub-specialty in private practice. Couples interacting with the therapist together have the opportunity to confront and work on their problems with the help of the therapist. The therapist may identify issues with either person, which requires counseling on an individual basis. This can benefit their treatment as a couple. However, couple treatment works on the issues within the marriage.

Susan Matorin is a graduate of Columbia University School of Social Work. She is a social worker on the full time faculty of the Department of Psychiatry, Weill Cornell Medical College. She currently divides her time at New York Hospital Payne Whitney Clinic between clinical work in ambulatory care with individuals with serious psychiatric illnesses, and a private practice. She also teaches couple and family practice to psychiatric residents in training. Until recently, she taught "Social Work with Families" at the Columbia School of Social Work. Ms. Matorin is a board member of the Helen Rehr Center for Social Work Practice.

CHAPTER 5

CLINICAL SOCIAL WORK WITH LESBIAN, GAY, BISEXUAL, AND TRANSGENDER COUPLES

Israel Martinez, LCSW

Introduction

Social workers receive specific education and training in the area of cultural sensitivity which prepares them to provide skilled support and assistance to populations that have been victimized and discriminated against. Social workers are also attuned to the impact of social, cultural, and religious forces on individuals. These skills may be particularly useful to lesbian, gay, bisexual, and transgender (LGBT) couples.

The LGBT community has experienced unprecedented growth in visibility, social acceptance, and rights over the past decade in many parts of the world. In recent years, gay marriage has been legalized in a large percentage of the United States. Yet, there are still many inequalities and prejudices that this minority community must endure. Many state legislatures and governors have fought fiercely against rulings favorable to LGBT citizens. LGBT couples have the added stressor of trying to maintain healthy relationships in the midst of intolerance.

Some issues that tend to be unique to LGBT couples include: 1) internalized homophobia or transphobia, causing low self-esteem in at least one partner, not allowing for a healthy intimate connection; 2) an increased need for attachment to others because their gender non-conforming behaviors as children were criticized and rejected; and 3) growing up without any model of what a non-heterosexual relationship should or could be. These issues will be briefly explored in this chapter.

Internalized Homophobia or Transphobia

An LGBT child growing up in a society or family that deems homosexuality or any deviation from the gender norm as "wrong," "evil," or "disgusting" will tend to believe that these descriptors are an accurate representation of who he or she is. It is difficult to repeatedly hear negative messages and see derogatory images about an aspect of oneself without feeling that they must contain some truth. This often leads to the internalization of these negative beliefs. Children are especially susceptible to taking in these cues and making them a part of their identity. Many LGBT couples have at least one partner who is experiencing some level of internalized homophobia or transphobia. Such feelings of self-hatred have the potential to get in the way of intimacy and connection because the person may feel as if he or she is not truly worthy of being loved or of being a person who provides love to someone else.

A clinical social worker is able to help a couple through this by taking time with each partner to realize, actively identify, and label negative stereotypes about the LGBT community and those beliefs that have been internalized.

Discussion then can center on the impact of these labels on the individual and the relationship. The social worker identifies these irrational beliefs and helps the couple view these beliefs from a reality perspective. Cognitive Behavior Therapy (CBT) is one technique that clinical social workers may use to help with this process. CBT is a form of treatment that uses a client's rational, cognitive thought processes to modify his or her irrational, dysfunctional thought patterns and thus improve coping mechanisms. An effective CBT exercise asks clients to write down the evidence for and against a certain belief. Often after completing the exercise, clients are able to see that there is more evidence against the way they were thinking than they have allowed themselves to be cognizant of. Seeing this on paper and going through the intellectual and emotional process of writing helps to break down unrealistic negative beliefs, freeing up the client to love and to be loved. This is a process that takes place over time.

Insecure Sense of Attachment

Children need to receive continuous validation from their parents in order to understand that their parents think they are smart, funny, attractive, and a pleasure to be around.

Children require the warmth of a hug and the assurance of love that comes from a kiss. Having these needs met by their parents helps children to realize they are worthy individuals and allows for secure bonds to form between them and their parents. This sense of security makes it easier to establish future healthy relationships with others. If instead, for example, a young boy's parents attempt to correct or ridicule him for playing with dolls, wearing his sister's dress, or crying too much, or if a young girl is criticized for not being "feminine" enough, refusing to wear frills, or being a "tomboy", their needs go unmet and their chances to create a secure bond with their parents are greatly reduced. They then may grow up desperately in need of attachment throughout life, but lacking a model of how to form secure attachments with others. In an intimate relationship, this desperation and lack of skill can lead to the person always wanting more from his or her partner in order to feel safe in the relationship and trying to get these needs met in unhealthy ways that wind up being destructive to the relationship. Some of these behaviors may include criticizing a partner for not doing enough to show his or her love, making unreasonable demands on a partner's time, or retreating from the relationship in order to avoid feeling any further hurt.

To help a couple dealing with conflicts that appear to be the result of insecure attachment, a clinical social worker will perform a thorough assessment of childhood development to see where the breaks in attachment may have occurred. The social worker will help the client to realize that his or her feelings are normal and that his or her struggles to feel secure and connected in the current relationship may be due to being deprived of certain needs during childhood and never having been taught how to connect with someone in a healthy manner. The worker will then teach effective communication skills to the couple so that each member is able to get his or her needs met and feel safe in the relationship.

Many clinical social workers are trained in a number of different techniques. One method to enhance effective communication between clients is to encourage one partner to share his or her feelings of insecurity (as opposed to solely accusing the other partner of wrongdoing). The other partner then repeats what was said so the person feels heard and validated for his or her experience.

Working without a Model

Whether healthy or unhealthy, most heterosexual couples have had some sort of model of what an intimate relationship should resemble. From these models they have received a guide for what roles to take in a relationship and what is deemed by society as constituting a "real" family. LGBT couples are unlikely to have a model of what it means to be in a non-heterosexual relationship. This translates into confusion over roles and the legitimacy of the relationship. For example, who does the cooking? Who takes out the trash? While these roles are less defined by gender today than they were in generations past, many households still use historical gender guidelines when deciding who does what. For someone who has struggled with his or her sexual orientation or gender identity, it can be extremely anxiety provoking to deal with not knowing what role to play or to try to resolve whether a role is "too feminine" or "too masculine" to embrace. This internal struggle can easily make its way into the relationship through arguments around household responsibilities and partners not contributing fairly to the household because they feel certain chores or responsibilities do not fit with their identity.

What Constitutes a Family?

Even with the proliferation of marriage equality, many LGBT couples today did not grow up understanding what makes up a family if there is not a mother, a father, and children. Can two women in a committed relationship be considered a family? What about a man and a woman if one is transgender? These couples already have inherent, built-in doubts about the stability of their relationship because they do not necessarily see themselves as a couple or a family, and those around them, including their own parents and siblings, may not acknowledge them as such. These doubts tend to make it more difficult for an LGBT couple to commit to the work needed to maintain a healthy relationship.

A clinical social worker would likely help a couple dealing with these role and perception issues to understand that what they are experiencing is normal because they did not have a model from which to learn. The clinician could then work with each partner to parse out the strengths and talents of each regarding household work, separate from what society deems acceptable for their gender. Based on that exploration, a structured plan for chores based on these strengths and talents can be established by the couple. The clinical social worker will, from the onset of treatment, use questions and phrasing that acknowledges them as a family, which can help the couple feel more secure and accepted. The worker will also guide the couple in exploring the pros and cons of advocating for others to see them as a family as well.

Case Example: Intimacy Issues

Andrew and Bill had been together for seven years when they decided to seek professional help from a clinical social worker around issues of intimacy in order to have a chance at salvaging their relationship. Their social worker spent the first session with the couple together in order to: 1) connect with both men as a couple, so as not to align with one partner over the other, 2) hear why they entered into therapy, 3) assess what might be causing the issues they would like to work on, and 4) have them agree on and commit to shared goals to improve the relationship.

During the initial session the couple shared a concern that when Andrew wanted to be intimate with his partner (from hand holding to sex), Bill would often shy away from his gestures and make some comment to demean himself or the importance of intimacy between the two men. They agreed this was something they wanted to work on because Andrew craved intimacy and Bill, in addition to wanting Andrew to be happy, also admitted to some desire for more intimacy in the relationship.

The next two sessions were individual sessions for each partner. This allowed the clinical social worker to gain a better understanding of what each partner was experiencing in the relationship and allowed Bill and Andrew the freedom to share issues of concern in therapy that they may not have wanted to say in front of one another. In Bill's session he talked about having grown up in Cuba, knowing he was different from other boys because he was gay, and feeling that this difference made him "evil." He described his family's strong religious beliefs and how they spoke in negative ways about homosexuals, often saying they were "filthy" and "worthless." In addition to this view of homosexuals at home, Bill's only exposure to openly gay men was to those who were harassed and living in poor conditions in his home town. This was all he knew about people who were gay and so he learned to believe that he was evil, worthless, and did not deserve to prosper in life. Although Bill became a successful adult and was able to experience more positive images and a more comprehensive understanding of what it meant to be gay, his initial beliefs from childhood were still ingrained in him. When exploring how this might be connected to his lack of wanting to be intimate with Andrew, Bill was able to see that a part of him felt that as a gay man he was not worthy of love from someone else. Bill was given the task, in session and at home, of writing down evidence for and against his belief that he was not worthy of Andrew's love. He was able to immediately realize that this thinking was irrational. Therapy helped him to begin to understand these thoughts as false beliefs. Bill worked hard to notice when he was having these negative thoughts and in the moment, to himself, learned to speak the evidence he had written down against these negative beliefs.

Andrew helped in the process by patiently alerting Bill when he was shying away from intimacy and by being supportive of Bill's struggles. In addition to teaching these skills, the worker was careful to explore barriers that might keep Bill stuck in his old patterns of thinking and explained the importance of practice and patience because Bill was working to undo a lifetime of believing in specific irrational thoughts and self-hate. Together, following this process, the couple was able to eventually increase the frequency and quality of their intimacy.

Conclusion

No relationship is easy and all healthy relationships take work. The unique challenges inherent in LGBT relationships require an increased expertise and sensitivity to gay and transgender issues on the part of any professional seeking to help LGBT couples. While the focus here was on clinical social workers, social workers in any area who may interact with such couples—from hospitals, to adoption agencies, to schools—are able to use their education and training, at the very least, to acknowledge LGBT couples as valid families and assess their specific needs.

Israel Martinez, LCSW focuses on the needs of the LGBT community. He received a Master of Science in Social Work at Columbia University and has provided mental health services to the LGBT community for over 10 years, including positions at the Lesbian, Gay, Bisexual &

Transgender Community Center, Gay Men's Health Crisis (GMHC), and the New York City Gay and Lesbian Anti-Violence Project. Mr. Martinez currently has a private practice in Montclair, NJ that specializes in therapy for LGBT clients. He feels that being open about one's sexual orientation is important in working with the LGBT community.

CHAPTER 6

CLINICAL SOCIAL WORKERS IN PRIVATE PRACTICE

Phyllis Caroff, PhD, LCSW, and Patsy Turrini, MSW, LCSW

Introduction

Social workers in private practice, like those working in agency or health care settings, are trained to assist people with a range of personal problems based on an understanding of the psychological, social, biological and/or economic factors that affect people's lives. As sole proprietors, they have greater flexibility than agency social workers and can set their own schedules and, in some instances, choose their own areas of specialization.[4] Like their colleagues in agencies, they are guided by their

---

[4]In essentially all situations, the social worker carries liability and malpractice insurance.

education in clinical skills and are responsible for maintaining current standards of professional social work, counseling, and psychotherapy practiced within legal and ethical conditions in a private office space. Private practitioners usually work with a network of other practitioners for consultation about problematic situations and to keep abreast of new ideas in practice.[5]

Social workers are committed to understanding the persons seeking help and the causes of their problems. As the therapist/client relationship develops, feelings of trust and safety develop and both parties come to understand the multiple factors creating difficulties for the client. Some of the problems for which people seek help can be relationships with friends or family or at the workplace, a troubled situation between parent and child, an individual's personal self-defeating patterns, or underdeveloped education and training.

---

[5]Private practitioners may or may not accept insurance fees or reduced or graduated fees based on income.

Areas of Specialization

Clinical social workers in private practice may develop specialties along with their basic preparation and the generic tools they use. Drawing from a myriad of current theories and research, each practitioner develops her or his own practice style and specialties. Some areas of specialization include psychotherapy or counseling for individual concerns; marital and family groups; parent-child troubled situations; child and adolescent issues; bereavement groups; geriatric services; divorce mediation, and/or career counseling.

The Goals of Treatment

Treatment is designed to ameliorate difficulties and establish new skills and choices for the client. The social worker and the persons(s) seeking relief set up goals for the therapeutic and counseling work. The client's development of a more solid sense of self-worth, self-respect, and self-regard are common goals. Treatment may also seek to optimize personal growth and freedom. In the ongoing work, clients develop new ways to handle problems and to give up self-defeating behavior. The clinical social worker in private practice works with clients to change habits and patterns of responding to life's challenges and opportunities.

Treatment may include the recalling of the painful past. Acknowledging pain and examining the past often helps clients resolve difficult issues and enhance their self-worth. Clients become empowered to feel more capable and to become more productive and more creative in their lives. The social worker assists the client to gain an inner sense of self-sufficiency and autonomy, the ability to plan, anticipate, and to be self-protective and self-soothing.

Additional goals might include freedom from excessive fears, grief, depression, or guilt that one is alive and a loved one is not (survivor guilt). Helping clients learn to understand others' needs and feelings, in addition to their own, protects them in social, family, and work situations. Improved problem solving and the ability to develop creative solutions are also goals.

If the client has problematic personal patterns, such as excessive rage and anger, self-belittling, sleep disturbance, or lack of productivity, the treatment goals are to modify and work to eliminate these difficulties. Self-understanding and self-acceptance is central to good health and a positive outcome of the work.

Accepting, appreciating, and working with our emotions are a great benefit that the treatment with a social worker can provide. Ours is a culture that shuns the display of feelings such as sadness, grief, loneliness, fear of death, hurt, humiliation, and anger. Even expressions of joy and happiness may be condemned in some families. If we set our emotions aside, they can accumulate and eventually produce physical symptoms such as depression, or erupt in family, social, or work settings. Discovering which experiences trigger these emotions, bringing them into acceptable form to the client, and creating a way for the emotions to be explained and managed is another valuable outcome of good treatment. Kindness and empathy can also be developed as a part of good clinical social work.

Another problem that women sometimes face is recovery from childbirth, which can be complicated and traumatic. A social worker can provide appropriate help to a client dealing with post-partum depression and/or a feeling of helplessness. New parents are often confused or frightened by normal developmental patterns or changes in their babies or young children and find that information about childrearing is very helpful to them.

Social workers are also sought out by people seeking help in handling illness. When illness becomes part of the daily life experience in the family, it may cause havoc in the household. Many resources may be needed to help, and one of the exceptional qualities of social workers, as compared to some of the other therapeutic professions, is that they are adept at finding needed services and resources for their clients.

Grief and loneliness set off by the death of a close person, such as a spouse, parent, child, or dear friend, will at times be overwhelming and many people are best served in a setting where they are free to talk about their feelings without disapproval or censure. Social work treatment, often in a small group of others who are grieving, for example, can be useful at these times.

The Clinician's Self-Awareness

Clinical social workers are expected to examine their own behavior and thinking. If a client does not make progress, social workers are obliged to consult with appropriate experts, or refer the client to other therapists. Self-examination is a requirement of the clinical social worker providing good care. At the same time, the person coming for help is encouraged to explore and evaluate if they are feeling better and if they feel they are getting the help they need.

Continuity of Connection and Safe Haven

Clinical social workers in private practice can control their use of time, workspace, and the continuity of care and relationship. They can set their own hours, and be available on a flexible schedule. The number of sessions with clients and the decision to continue or terminate are not defined by an agency, and can be decided by the social worker and the client. When a bond and feeling of safety has been established, clients can work, finish, leave when ready, and return if they want to. Some clients keep contact for a lifetime, others come for a short period, while others leave and return when they feel the need. This is a distinctive feature of the private social work practice, depending on the client's personal resources and/or insurance coverage. By and large this flexibility is not possible in agency settings, where organizational rules and protocols may dictate the length of treatment.

Case Example: Returning for Help

Warren had worked with a clinical social worker many years earlier around difficult marital issues. After a divorce he lived some years as a single man, eventually remarried, and became very successful in his work.

Fifteen years later, he called the social worker. He was now struggling with Parkinson's disease, a neurological disorder affecting the central nervous system.

When he walked into her room again, he felt at home; it was just the same as it had been in prior years; like he 'never left it'. That alone helped him to begin to feel more comfortable. He spent three months exploring the changes in his life and the future; his wife also came to some sessions. In the course of these three months of treatment, he adapted to his disability. He felt more stable and better able to master his life and handle his fears. When the social worker planned to be away on vacation, she called him to let him know she would be away for three weeks, and told him when she would be back so they could resume treatment. Had he called when she was away without this knowledge, his anxiety could have been exacerbated and aggravated his condition. Her attention to his need for connection reinforced his awareness of her constancy and that she intended to return.

Warren's situation demonstrates the return to a safe place to get help and a growth- promoting relationship. He could connect his deepest concerns, the shock of the illness, which had disrupted his life, and gain new ideas and perspectives on how to move forward.

Volunteer Services by Private Practitioners: The Soldiers Project

A social worker in private practice has the flexibility to provide free services or services at a reduced rate. A number of clinical social workers in private practice volunteer to provide free counseling to soldiers and their families who have been in Iraq and Afghanistan. This service is known as the Soldiers Project. Members of the military are often reluctant to obtain help, fearful that a paper trail recording their use of mental health services might be discovered through military insurance or health records. The privacy of the social worker's work, in a private office without connection to the military bureaucracy or insurance companies, allows for the soldier's full disclosure of personal problems and needs, without documentation, which reduces the threats of retribution or fear of exposure.

Separations from family members can create deep, sometimes overwhelming anxiety for those in the armed services. Deployments inevitably stir old and new fears. Airing their battle traumas in the psychotherapy/counseling sessions allows for repair, easing of anxiety and the development of new thought patterns.

Struggling with Anxiety and Grief

Many people (young and old) are isolated due to lack of family nearby, no family at all. If they have not developed a roster of trusted friends or a social world that can support them they can feel very lonely and isolated. Perhaps organizations they know and work places are so toxic that they cause pain and anguish and people have no place to be supported or understood. Depression and anxiety may follow. Many people in these kinds of situations may seek professional help to work on the underlying reasons for their feelings of sadness and pain.

Case Example: Mrs. M

Mrs. M found her clinical social worker's name through her insurance plan. She described feeling depressed and fatigued, was somewhat overweight, and working sporadically with long hours in a difficult environment where she was not respected. She got dizzy at work. Family life was grim and joyless. Though she was separated from a physically dangerous man, and though he lived in a different area, she still feared him and felt he could hunt her down; she did not want to file for a divorce, lest he find her. She was living with another partner, with three adolescent children, none of whom were maturing at the normal rate. Moreover her only son had been killed nine years earlier in an automobile accident. Though she had attended grief groups, she was in despair and mourning, and unforgiving of herself about his death.

Mrs. M was without a steady income or pension, but was willing to explore a referral for vocational counseling to acquire new skills. Her feelings of lack of entitlement to a decent life emanated from many sources, including the psychological wounds of the prior domestic violence that still haunted her, and she felt chronic despair.

During the course of her treatment, she began to take better care of her health; lost weight, left the toxic job, and improved her relationships with those around her. Her nightmares lessened. She expressed interest in continuing her therapeutic work in the future.

Conclusion

Private practitioners address a broad spectrum of individual emotional problems and issues. They typically have greater flexibility than agency representatives, but must abide by the code of ethics of the social work profession. They might be right for you or a family member or friend struggling with a problem.

Phyllis Caroff, PhD, LCSW, is Professor Emerita, Hunter College School of Social Work. She taught casework and clinical practice courses in both the master's and doctoral programs and has published extensively in clinical practice and health care. She was the designer and director of the Post-Master's Certificate Program in Advanced Clinical Social Work. Professor Caroff was awarded an Honorary Doctorate in Humane Letters by Hunter College in January, 1995. Currently, she is in private practice in New York. She is a member of the board of the Helen Rehr Center for Social Work Practice.

Patsy Turrini, LCSW is a clinical social worker and psychoanalyst in private practice in Nassau County, New York.

PART II

Specialized Areas of Practice

CHAPTER 7

SOCIAL WORK IN THE TREATMENT OF ADDICTION

Janet Lerner, PhD, LCSW

Introduction

Social workers have played an important role in addiction treatment for the last 50 years. Bachelor's and Master's degree-level social workers have been employed in addiction treatment programs as senior administrators, clinical directors, and case managers. The field of addiction treatment and the standards of social work fit very well together. For example, three of the most important values of the social work profession include meeting clients where they are, empowering clients to be part of their own healing process, and supporting clients as they move from treatment to recovery. All of these values are used in the treatment of addiction.

In assessing clients for treatment, the social worker seeks to identify what is going on with the client at the present time ("meeting the client where he/she is now"), and whether and how the client wants to begin the process of "empowerment" – taking control of her or his own situation – which is so important to recovery. Social workers focus on empowerment because we understand that we cannot "fix" people struggling with an addiction. However, we can help them develop the tools and make the changes needed so that they can "fix" themselves.

What social workers can do is help clients understand their situation, their decision-making process, what tends to influence that process, and how to develop an effective plan to protect themselves from the things that trigger relapse and drug use. The social worker can also address trauma, which is one of the major causes of addiction and relapse. Effective trauma counseling helps the person struggling with addiction address the feelings (such as anxiety, fear, shame, guilt, grief, or anger) that cause him or her to turn to drugs or other addictions to cope. Using drugs or alcohol to relieve the pain of such emotions is often referred to as "self-medicating." Treatment for trauma, which may be the source of those painful emotional states, is an important aspect of all addiction treatment, and many master's degree-level clinical social workers have training in this area.

Social workers typically have some training in family therapy as well. In order to help addicted people, it is critical to help them understand how to deal with family members who unknowingly may trigger or reinforce their negative behaviors. Many substance abusers may live in a family where addiction is already present. The family system of addiction is a closed system that typically sustains a continuation of addictive behaviors. It creates specific roles for individuals within the family, such as scapegoat, enabler, doer, hero, mascot, and/or loner. If one of these individuals tries to get help and change his or her behavior, the family system becomes out of balance, and members of the family will intentionally or unintentionally do whatever they can to bring that person back into their assigned role.

Case Example: Family Members Undermining an Addict's Treatment

One client agreed, after much encouragement, to enter a 28-day inpatient rehabilitation program to get his drug and alcohol use under control. He lived with his family, who were all using alcohol and other drugs and treated him as a scapegoat for their problems, and he was constantly relapsing in spite of his strong commitment to sobriety. The social worker had a strong relationship with him, and was able to convince him that getting away from the family would help him get sober, and that he needed to find other living arrangements so that he could have a productive and meaningful life.

About a week after entering rehab, his family came to visit him. All of his family members had been drinking and clearly wanted to bring him back into the family where he could resume the role of the family scapegoat. After this incident, the social worker helped the client analyze the experience and overcome the embarrassment he felt so that he could continue to stay in rehab and complete his effort to separate from his family. He did stay, and ultimately he was able to move away from his family. He found employment in a recovery program and found housing far from the neighborhood where his family lived. He maintained a drug-free life thereafter.

As seen in this particular example, the family's efforts to return the recovering addict to a state of active drug and/or alcohol use is strong when the 'scapegoat' tries to quit doing drugs or stop other addictive behaviors. On a subconscious level the family members fear that if anything changes, the family will fall apart. Social workers, who understand the functioning of the family, also understand how important it is to anticipate the difficulties addicted clients may face. Social workers help clients understand how to handle these challenges without isolating themselves and/or repeating this kind of family system. Clients have a greater likelihood of success in their efforts to overcome addiction if they identify and overcome the risky behaviors most likely to cause relapse. They are also less likely to hand down to their children and grandchildren the disease of addiction and all of the difficulties it entails.

Addiction and the Law

The harsh treatment of addiction by our criminal justice system creates problems for those who struggle with substance abuse; many often end up incarcerated. Some face a variety of legal problems once they leave prison, including severe family problems, back-due child support, and difficulty finding a job due to their criminal records. Clients also often struggle with poverty, racism, and discrimination, which increase their barriers to re-entry into society after being in jail.

Social workers are trained to deal with the holistic range of problems clients face, and can use that hands-on approach to assist with those problems of formerly incarcerated persons suffering from addiction. They can help substance abusers obtain legal representation from public defenders and other low- income legal services providers. Help with parenting skills and treatment for family issues and trauma are other ways in which social workers can help former substance abusers make the transition from incarceration to living in the community.

Evidence-based Practice and Addiction Treatment

In "evidence-based practice," social workers use techniques that have been tested in rigorous research studies and proven effective. There are three evidence-based treatment modalities that social workers use with good results in treating people struggling with addiction. These are reflective or empathic listening, motivational interviewing, and cognitive-behavioral therapy. We will briefly explore each of these methods over the following pages.

Reflective or empathic listening is a technique that involves listening closely to the client, summarizing the client's thoughts in the listener's own words to determine if she or he actually understood what the client was trying to say, and thus setting the stage for further communication between them. When done well, the social worker empathizes with the client and lets the client know she is being heard, understood, and perhaps even accepted. Addicted clients rarely get affirmation for talking about their problems. This modality is an excellent tool for social workers who are working with those who have struggled to feel respected and need to be affirmed. Empathetic listening establishes a basis of trust and enables the work on getting the addictive behavior under control to move forward.

Case Example: Reflective, Empathetic Listening

A client is talking about all of the negative things people say to her about her drug use and other addiction-supporting behaviors. She has entered into prostitution to try to support herself and her habit. Rather than judging or suggesting ways the client can change that behavior, the social worker establishes a connection with the client in her current frame of mind, and sets a tone of empathy and understanding by reflecting the client's comments back to her, and highlighting the client's concerns. The social worker says things like: "You seem to be experiencing a lot of criticism from others" or "You seem to feel that your life is getting more out of control as you get involved in things you were not doing before" or "It sounds like you have little or no support in a very difficult and unhappy situation." This helps the client frame the multiple worries on her mind, which is the starting point for gaining control over her dysfunctional behavior.

Motivational Interviewing is a technique in which the social worker assists the client to find her or his own internal motivation for change by identifying, exploring, and trying to understand his or her own ambivalence about the dysfunctional (addictive) behavior. It is extremely effective with addiction clients. It helps clients identify for themselves the areas where there is a need for change and growth and the resources they have available in overcoming addiction. It helps clients see that they can talk about their issues without being disrespected. Their problems can be solved with the help of additional resources and a consistent, committed effort. The supportive aspects of motivational interviewing enable clients to feel, often for the first time, that they are not alone in their efforts to overcome the past and move forward into recovery.

Case Example: Motivational Interviewing

Manny was struggling with addiction after a car accident. He had been put on opiates as part of his pain management treatment. After several weeks of use he was taken off the medication, but he found that he could not tolerate the pain of withdrawal. He felt very ashamed and thought that if he went to treatment his life would be ruined. People would look down on him, and everybody would think of him as a junkie.

Using motivational interviewing, Manny's social worker stated, "I can see that you feel a desire to get help, and to stop using the drug. However, you are afraid that if you go to a treatment program, that information will get out to your friends and colleagues. Then people will start talking about you, avoiding you, and generally disrespecting you. That would be too much for you to handle. What other options do you have to deal with the addiction?"

The social worker helped Manny look at the difficulties he now had to go through in order to obtain the drugs. Manny began to explore his options to avoid using drugs. The social worker began to carefully help Manny develop a possible action plan, which could hopefully lead to his treatment and recovery. They discussed a three-day hospitalization for detoxification, and if needed, possible counseling through an outpatient or substance abuse treatment program which he was able to consider.

Cognitive Behavioral Therapy (CBT) is a form of treatment that explores the client's thinking patterns that lead to self-destructive actions and the beliefs that direct these thoughts. It uses the client's rational, cognitive thought processes to modify the irrational, dysfunctional thought patterns and improve their coping mechanisms. This allows the patient and the therapist to search for patterns in their thinking that can cause them to have negative thoughts which can lead to negative feelings and self-destructive behaviors. It is a comprehensive approach to counseling that enables addicted clients to develop coping skills to help them through the difficult times they face in establishing and sustaining recovery. It offers them the opportunity to talk about what has happened to them in the past as well as the problems they are experiencing in the present. As they talk about their difficulties, they are able to see more clearly which past experiences have caused them to doubt their chances of success and their ability to work toward recovery. They can learn how to quickly identify issues before problem behaviors take over and ruin good opportunities.

The most important aspect of cognitive behavioral therapy is that the addicted client learns what he or she is doing that causes problems, understands that these things are learned behaviors, and is able to change decisions which are not helpful. Clients begin to understand what they need to achieve for growth and healthy living. Hopefully, the past can no longer control the present or destroy their future.

Many addicted clients are also at risk for co-occurring disorders – in addition to the substance abuse or addiction, they may be suffering from depression, anxiety, or a mental illness. They must be screened carefully for these disorders before being treated for the addiction alone. Cognitive behavioral therapy is an excellent tool that can help those with co-occurring disorders become more functional and capable.

Case Example: Using CBT with a Client Suffering from Drug Addiction and Schizophrenia

One patient came to a program with symptoms of schizophrenic hallucinations that were interfering with her recovery and functioning. She held an important position in a government agency and had a master's degree in psychology, but she was not able to control the hallucinations or the paranoia caused by her disorder. Using cognitive behavioral techniques, her social worker began to address the hallucinations and help her develop ways of determining whether what she was seeing was real or not. With ongoing support, and the use of prescribed medications, she was able to maintain her job, stop using drugs, and function without being controlled by her disorder.

Case Example: Using CBT with a Client Suffering from Alcoholism and Trauma

Gloria is involved with alcohol abuse, and as her social worker interviews her it becomes evident that there is a traumatic issue, childhood sexual abuse, that is feeding the alcohol abuse. In one session, Gloria talks about how she was in a movie theatre and she smelled something that reminded her of her abuser. Even though the abuse had happened more than 15 years ago, Gloria became very frightened and had to fight to stay seated in the theater as she really wanted to run out. She was able to use a mindful relaxation technique, deep breathing, and settle her panic

attack long enough to think about where she was, how
unlikely that her abuser would be in the theater, and what
other explanations she could give for the scent. She was
able to relax, watch the movie, leave the theater after she
was finished, and not have any more panic or anxiety once
she took the tools she had learned from cognitive
behavioral therapy and applied them to this situation.

Conclusion

Social workers value the integrity of the individual, and respect their clients' ability to live healthier and more productive lives. Starting where the client is means understanding what the client is dealing with now and recognizing that change is a difficult struggle. Using motivational interviewing and cognitive behavioral therapy, supported by reflective listening, makes that struggle much easier. It gives the addicted client the feeling that there may actually be someone who understands and cares, and that is the first step to entering recovery.

Social workers have unique skills to work with clients with addiction. They can help to identify what is really needed, and link the client to the resources available within the community. They can also advocate for clients when necessary. This makes a difference for addicted individuals who have felt powerless and hopeless for so much of their lives. The addicted client feels supported by the work of the social worker on his or her behalf, and begins to feel the effort they need to make may be worth it after all.

Dr. Janet Lerner has been in the field of addiction treatment since 1973, and has been the Administrator of Research, Development and Training at Narco Freedom, Inc., since 1988. In 2003 she received an additional appointment as Executive Director of Damon House New York, Inc. Dr. Lerner is a graduate of Ohio State University (BSSW and MA) and Columbia University School of Social Work (PhD and Post-doctorate). She is on the faculties of the Alliance Theological Seminary Graduate School of Counseling, and the Columbia School of Social Work as an adjunct faculty member. Dr. Lerner heads Restoration and Healing, Inc. which is a small private not-for-profit and NGO registered with the United Nations. She has published several books and articles on sexual abuse and family violence.

CHAPTER 8

SOCIAL WORK WITH INDIVIDUALS AND FAMILIES AFFECTED BY ALZHEIMER'S DISEASE OR A RELATED DEMENTIA

Matt Kudish, LMSW

Introduction

There arc approximately one hundred different underlying causes of the state of mind known as dementia. Some causes are treatable and reversible; most are not. The most common irreversible causes of dementia include Alzheimer's disease, vascular dementia, Lewy body dementia, and front temporal dementias. Delineating these complexities can be challenging, even when qualified medical professionals are involved.

Obtaining a diagnosis is just the first step in an often complicated and exceedingly emotional journey. *The*

emotional impact of dementia with symptoms of extreme
forgetfulness and inability to recognize family members
and their surroundings cannot be overstated.

Doctors are neither trained nor, in most cases, prepared to provide support to the person with the disease or those involved in his or her care around the non-medical aspects of the illness. This is where the expertise of trained social work professionals can be of particular value. They can provide the necessary information, education, and support to sustain the highest quality of life for the person living with the illness as well as everyone involved in his or her care.

The assistance and support social workers can provide can generally be grouped into four areas:

1. Disease education
2. Care plan development and implementation
3. Individual counseling
4. Family counseling

Disease Education

It's difficult, if not impossible, to read a newspaper or
watch the news (or read a book or watch a movie, for that
matter) and not see something about Alzheimer's disease or
other causes of dementia.

From theories around prevention to complicated definitions
of terms to misconceptions about disease progressions and
prognoses there is no shortage of information, and
misinformation, about dementia available to the public.

Very often people think they understand dementia, in large
part because it's rare to meet someone who has not heard of
dementia or been exposed to the disease through the media.
We may know someone who has the disease, read about it,
heard about a friend's experience, and think we know all we
need to know. If only it were that simple.

The challenge is that we don't know what we don't know.
And sometimes the belief that we have enough information
to make the best decisions is misinformed and can get in
the way of our moving forward in the best possible way,

creating further challenges that potentially could have been avoided.

Working with a social worker who specializes in this field can provide a solid, dependable foundation of knowledge that can inform all of the future decisions to be made.

In order to successfully manage the disease and its impact, we need to understand the nuances we are dealing with, and be open to learning best practices around the provision of care. The more we know, the better prepared we are for what is to come. Knowledge, as the saying goes, is power.

Given the variety and large number of causes of dementia, and the vast number of similarities and differences that can exist between them, it is most important to have as much specific information and knowledge as possible of the particular individual and family receiving care.

Social workers can impart the basic foundation of knowledge around the specific disease and build on that foundation with skills around best practices in regard to providing the highest quality of care, increasing the likelihood of a better quality of life for both the person with the disease and everyone involved in his or her care.

Self-care is also often foreign to us, or at least secondary. In addition, there are skills that can be taught and learned that, when implemented, can make it easier, enhancing quality of life for both the person with the disease and those involved in his or her care, an important part of the whole care system.

Social workers can provide the necessary disease information and education to provide the foundation of knowledge individuals and families need to build upon in order to adequately and appropriately plan and care for the person with dementia, and themselves.

Case Example: Disease Education

Karen is the primary caregiver for her father, Al, who has been recently diagnosed with Alzheimer's disease. Karen meets with a social worker to learn more about the disease, including what she can expect over time, and the resources that are available for both her father and herself. During their meeting, the social worker walks Karen through

Alzheimer's as a disease process, explaining the way the disease manifests inside the brain. This information provides Karen with a deeper understanding as to why her father is saying and doing the things he is. Understanding the way her father's disease is developing in his brain better enables Karen to be more patient and empathic, and to manage her expectations for the future. The social worker explains the common symptoms one can expect throughout the spectrum of Alzheimer's disease, and provides information for Karen to be mindful of when she is interacting with, or arranging activities and care for, her father.

Care Plan Development & Implementation

If you've met one person with dementia, you've met one person. This makes developing a care plan an entirely unique undertaking and requires a focus on the individual situation in which you find yourself. There is no one-size-fits-all approach to dementia care.

With this in mind, social workers who are experts in dementia can play a vital role in ensuring the needs of the person with the disease, and those involved in his or her care, can be met in a meaningful way.

When confronted with a disease that results in dementia, it can be incredibly difficult to know what to do, and when. Upon diagnosis there are myriad issues to be addressed, but prioritizing them appropriately, and following through on each of them, can be an enormously complicated undertaking. For example, if a loved one is very forgetful and seemingly confused about time or location, this can be the time to seek professional help.

Legal and financial planning is an important component of any care plan related to dementia. A good first step in legal and financial planning is to complete a series of documents referred to as advance directives. Advance directives include the health care proxy, power of attorney and, in some states, the living will. Social workers can help you better understand what these documents are, their meaning, how they work together, and how to complete them in a timely fashion while engaging the person with the disease as much as possible.

Legal and financial planning also requires a thorough understanding of the finances of the person with dementia, as well as other potential resources that may be available to assist in covering costs related to care. This planning can inform the family and caregivers about public benefits and/or entitlements that can be applied for or obtained to help with the provision, and in some cases the cost, of care. Social workers are trained experts at assisting people in successfully navigating these complex systems. Of course, some legal and financial planning will likely involve working with an elder law attorney, a legal expert in this area. Social workers with experience in dementia care may also be able to provide referrals to such persons, and help families better understand how to be good consumers of legal services in terms of knowing what questions to ask and how to prepare for consultations to get the most out of them.

Safety planning—including driving, home safety (locks, stove, baths) and wandering—is another essential component of the care plan. Other issues that will likely be addressed during care planning sessions include how the person spends his or her time, connecting the person with dementia to community resources to remain socially engaged, and helping those involved in the person's care best understand the person's needs, and how to anticipate them throughout the trajectory of the illness.

Once a plan is developed, social workers can be instrumental in supporting family and other resources as they begin to operationalize the plan. This includes assisting people in navigating the often complicated systems with which it is often necessary to engage, as well as the barriers that all too often present themselves. Social workers specializing in geriatrics and/or dementia have the experience and skills necessary to successfully negotiate this often complex journey.

Recognizing that dementia affects individuals and families in different ways, it is likely that along your journey the care plan will need to be revisited or, at the very least, tweaked to accommodate changes in the person's illness or the family's situation.

Case Example: Care Plan Development

Now that Karen has a more solid understanding about Alzheimer's disease, her social worker can support her by building on that foundational knowledge and exploring some of the more concrete aspects of Karen's caregiving role and responsibilities toward her father, Al. While Al is in the early stage of Alzheimer's disease, Karen's social worker has explained the progressive and degenerative nature of Alzheimer's and, as such, the importance of beginning to plan for how to make sure Al's needs are met today and continue to be met in the future. The social worker talks with Karen about how Al spends his time, and explores with her opportunities for Al to remain engaged in activities that bring him pleasure despite his diagnosis. The social worker supports Karen in helping to identify and investigate programs for people in the early stage of the disease to provide Al with opportunities to remain active and engaged socially and physically. Companion services are explored to see where Al might benefit from additional support as well as someone to accompany him to museums and baseball games, two of his favorite activities.

The social worker also explores with Karen the legal and financial aspects of Al's diagnosis. Again, recognizing the progressive nature of Alzheimer's, the social worker provides referrals to elder law attorneys who can help the family negotiate important documents like a health care proxy and power of attorney. These documents provide Al with the opportunity to speak to who he wants to make health care decisions should the time come when he can no longer do so independently, as well as the kinds of decisions that he would like made in that situation. Families are often reluctant to have these kinds of discussions and a social worker can support the family in becoming more prepared to bring up these more sensitive topics as well as follow through on completing the action items related to them. The social worker reminds Karen that there is a limited window of opportunity during which Al can—and should—participate actively in these discussions and decisions. The social worker also helps Karen understand that there are potentially serious consequences to not taking action on these issues as soon as possible. Some of these consequences would prevent the family from sheltering Al's income and resources in a way that enables him to access public benefits that can cover the costs associated with long term care, such as Medicaid. While some people are not eligible for Medicaid in their current state, social workers can assist families in becoming eligible by explaining the rules and regulations of these complicated systems and helping families negotiate through them. Having the benefit of a longer view,

Karen's social worker is able to pull the curtain back a bit on the future of Al's progression and help Karen and the family better prepare for what's to come, including ensuring Al is as safe as possible in his home so that he can remain in the community for as long as possible.

Individual Counseling

The emotional impact of living with a diagnosis or caring for a person with dementia cannot be overstated. No matter how hard we try, or how much we focus on the concrete aspects of the disease, the emotional piece can never be overlooked. And frankly, until we begin to process and explore the emotions involved we can hardly address the concrete needs in a meaningful way because the elephant in the room is simply occupying too much of our mental bandwidth.

Even when the focus is placed primarily on the concrete tasks associated with caring for a person, the emotional impact is profound. Social workers can help individuals affected by dementia begin to explore and process the emotions that go along with dealing with the disease.

From the onset of symptoms to the diagnosis to the insidious decline, emotional support is a vital component of successfully managing living with or caring for someone who has a dementing illness.

For those diagnosed in the early stage of the disease, counseling may be a particularly useful option to explore the complicated feelings around acknowledging and accepting an Alzheimer's diagnosis. Being able to talk with a social worker can be particularly helpful to the early stage individual as his or her world may feel as if it is falling apart. Some of the common issues that may come up for persons in the early stage may be whether, and how, to share the diagnosis with others, issues around work, driving, living alone, and planning for the future.

Social workers can help caregivers to reconcile their complicated feelings associated with caring for someone with a dementing illness. Referred to as the "Long Goodbye," caring for someone with dementia is often described as more complicated (multifaceted, multilayered) than caring for someone with other health conditions due to the duality of the illness--bringing about changes in the cognition of the person receiving care, while his or her physical needs become more complicated over time. Grieving the loss of the person as their disease progresses while at the same time being relied upon to provide more and more care to the person. Personality changes and behavior challenges often compound the emotional impact, as people with dementia can become more difficult to care for. These complications can lead to emotional difficulties for caregivers. The ability to speak with a social worker who understands the process and who can validate feelings can be incredibly helpful. Too often the disease is isolating for the person living with it and just as isolating for the caregiver, leaving people feeling alone in this journey,

The emotional support that social workers can provide can be a lifeline to more successfully dealing with the impact of the disease.

If you haven't been through this it may be difficult to understand the impact—in every imaginable way—that caring for someone with dementia will have on a person. Social workers can help the Alzheimer's patient and caregiver to be prepared to cope with the changes, accept them as they come, and sustain their ability to continue to care.

Case Example: Individual Counseling

Karen and her father Al have always been close. Karen's mother died when she was very young and her father raised her and her younger brother on his own. Growing up, Karen was always "daddy's little girl" and enjoyed the relationship that she and her father had. Now Karen is Al's primary caregiver, and she needs to attend to him in many ways in which she'd never had to before. Al relies on Karen to make sure there is food in his house, his bills are paid, medications are taken, and appointments kept. This role reversal has started to take a toll on Karen. Karen also has a partner and two children who need her time and attention, in addition to working full time. Balancing these competing priorities has been a struggle for Karen. Not to mention the emotional impact of seeing her father succumb to Alzheimer's disease—even in the early stage. She's mourning the loss of the man she's always known and struggling to come to terms with the ways in which he is able to be a part of her life despite his illness.

Karen is able to connect with her social worker to talk through some of these issues. Helping to normalize Karen's experience, and remind her that she is not alone can be a tremendous support for Karen during this very difficult time. Her social worker helps Karen prioritize and balance her own needs, and those of her family, with those of her father. Karen's social worker gives Karen permission to set appropriate boundaries with her father to ensure that her own needs are able to be met. Karen also feels frustrated by her brother, Teddy, and the fact that he doesn't do more to help with Al. Her social worker explores with Karen ways that she can attempt to engage her brother in a more meaningful way to better support herself and Al.

Family Counseling

Family dynamics can also complicate matters in the face of dementia and social workers can be instrumental in helping families get on the same page and move forward in the most effective way to ensure the person with the disease gets his or her needs met, with the least negative impact on the family.

As the disease progresses, roles often reverse, in cases where adult children are required to play the role of caregiver to their parent. In these situations, all involved may benefit from speaking with a social worker to explore what these changes mean and how to best make sure everyone's needs are being met as best they can.

Other family dynamic issues may include siblings who disagree about the kind of care a parent needs, or struggle with the fact that one sibling may be taking on more of the tasks related to care than other siblings. These situations can breed resentment or feelings of frustration that, if not dealt with, can do long term damage to the family relationships. In other cases, the person doing the majority of the caregiving may feel as if long distance or less hands-on caregivers are telling him or her what to do, which can also bring up complicated feelings that could get in the way of relationships. Issues around assets may also arise and cause complications among family members. In each of these situations, individual and/or family counseling with a social worker may prove helpful to explore these feelings or, perhaps, even resolve some of the tensions that exist.

Case Example: Family Counseling

Karen and her brother, Teddy, don't necessarily see eye to eye as it relates to Al, his disease, and his care needs. Karen sees Al much more often than Teddy and as such, she feels she has a better handle on what he needs. Teddy, who has never felt the same kind of closeness with Al as Karen, visits every other weekend to spend a few hours with his father. He feels that their dad is doing well and that Karen is overreacting. The fact that they aren't on the same page as it relates to Al and his needs is making it more complicated to get things done.

A social worker meets with the two of them to explore and better understand their individual perspectives and how these perspectives might be affecting Al. By meeting with a social worker, Karen and Teddy are each able to share their feelings about their dad, his needs, and how to best meet them on a prospective basis. The social worker helps to create an environment where honest sharing can occur between Karen and Teddy, and Karen is able to share with Teddy that she wishes he was helping her out with more of the day to day activities related to caring for Al. Teddy shares how difficult it is for him to be around his dad through these changes; how emotionally tough it is for him to see his dad declining.   The social worker helps Teddy better understand that Karen knows all too well what Teddy is going through and that they can be a support for each other.

Together, with the social worker's assistance, they negotiate what kinds of tasks Teddy could do that would not only give Karen a break, but also allow Teddy to spend more time with his father.   Teddy acknowledges that his schedule affords more flexibility than Karen's and as such, he agrees to play a more active role in making sure Al gets to his many doctor's appointments each month.   This alleviates anxiety for Karen, and likely means that she'll have to call out of work less often.   They also agree to communicate more with one another to ensure they're each doing okay emotionally, and that no resentment builds up between them.   They agree to set up another appointment with the social worker for the following month to touch base on how these new changes are going.

Conclusion

Individuals and families involved in caring for a person
with dementia will be better served if, over time, they are
able to accept changes as they come, recognize they cannot
do it alone, give up the idea of being the "perfect"
caregiver, understand their limitations, ask for—and
accept—help, and to take care of themselves. Each of these
is a process in and of themselves. With the help of a social
worker, they're all within reach.

*Matt Kudish, LMSW is the Senior Vice President of
Caregiver Services, CaringKind – The Heart of
Alzheimer's Caregiving.*

CHAPTER 9

SOCIAL WORK WITH DISABLED ADULTS AND THEIR CAREGIVERS

Frances Brennan, LCSW

Introduction

Social workers have long played a key role in helping adults with disabilities, whether they have a lifelong, chronic condition or a disability caused more recently by (for example) stroke, trauma, or age-related dementia. Social workers are trained to listen carefully to clients to ascertain the specifics of their problems, to encourage clients to become stronger where possible, to identify and facilitate referrals to other relevant, specialized resources, and to manage the complex relationships and problems that may arise between nursing homes or medical facilities and the client and his or her family or caregiver. The social work model uses a strength-based approach that focuses on treating the whole person with the right combination of interventions that suit the needs of the disabled person and his or her family members and caretakers.

This chapter describes the types of disabilities social workers address, the kinds of skilled assessments, counseling, referrals, and interventions they provide, and the critical role they play in seeking ways to maximize the care, comfort, and physical and psychological healing each particular individual can achieve.

Types of Disabilities

Different types of disabilities present different challenges. A person who suffers a brain injury may experience significant cognitive impairment, as well as speech deficits. He/she may also have difficulty with self-care because of the impairments. Some symptoms can be corrected with therapy, but improvement may be a very slow process.

People who have suffered a stroke commonly have physical impairments (difficulty walking, reaching, and impaired motor skills which make dressing, bathing and using the toilet difficult). In addition, after a stroke a person might have impaired speech as well as cognitive impairment. Rehabilitation can often help a person regain or compensate for their physical and cognitive losses.

Elderly people who appear confused or forgetful may have dementia, but family and caregivers should not assume this. Family and/or caregivers should first encourage the elderly person to have a physical examination and make sure the physician knows what medications he or she is using. Some medications can cause symptoms of dementia. In addition, mild cognitive impairment frequently accompanies aging, but is not dementia or Alzheimer's disease

People who are disabled because of trauma have to cope with the shock of the traumatic event as well as the physical and/or mental impairments. They may have to talk to police or other authorities who are investigating an accident or incident. Questioning may feel accusatory or victims may feel that they are responsible for what happened to them.

Treatments

Rehabilitation is a common treatment for the newly disabled as well as those with lifelong disabilities. Physical therapy helps a person with disabilities to maximize physical independence. The disabled may learn to walk again, walk with an assistive device, use a wheelchair independently, or to control some aspects of wheelchair use. People with longer-term disabilities are frequently reevaluated to see if there is any potential for improvement or to use a course of therapy to regain some physical skills that have declined.

Occupational therapy focuses on upper body strength. People with disabilities can learn to eat, drink, dress, bathe, and use the toilet either independently or with assistive devices.

Speech therapy is crucial after a stroke or brain injury to help a person relearn how to communicate. In many cases, a person can graduate from using a communication board used to spell out words to relearning normal speech.

Lifelong Disabilities

Adults with lifelong disabilities will likely have developed coping skills over time, but may be plagued with feelings of frustration over their physical dependence, fear of growing helplessness, and resentment that they have never experienced a normal life.

Case Example: Helping a Client with Polio Deal with Depression

The social worker from a community service agency met with a client with paralysis as a result of childhood polio. Her sister, who was concerned about her increased sadness and unwillingness to engage in activities, had referred her for counseling. The client answered routine questions with one-word responses and appeared tired and sad. She denied feelings of depression, and became angry at what she described as intrusive questions. The social worker responded to her anger with gentle support. The client went on to discuss her frustration with getting older and nothing changing for the better. Exploring her concerns, the social worker suggested that she consider consulting with a psychiatrist about medications for depression and meeting weekly with the social worker to talk about why she is frustrated and to explore possible services that she could utilize. The social worker explained that it is not uncommon to feel frustrated and angry when it seems nothing changes and that she would like to see if together they can find a way for her to move forward.

Social work interventions with people with disabilities include counseling which focuses on what the clients can do and how to mobilize their strengths. To identify these strengths, the social worker explores the client's background to identify how he or she coped with challenges earlier in life. The social worker might also seek medical information to better understand the depth of the disability and help the person develop realistic goals; he/she might also seek psychiatric consultation for the client to identify possible depression or other psychiatric issues.

Newly Acquired Disabilities

Adults recently disabled will experience depression as they mourn their lost physical ability, frustration as they begin to experience their limitations, shame if their disability involves help with personal care, and anger over the cause of the disability.

Case Example: Helping a Disabled Man Reach for Independence

A man who lost both legs in an automobile accident met with a social worker in the hospital to discuss discharge plans. The client stated he wanted to go to a veterans' hospital so he would not burden his family. He had refused rehabilitation because he thought his situation was hopeless. The social worker asked him about his experiences in the service. The client said it was ironic that he had survived Afghanistan only to be disabled a few years later. Over time, the social worker helped him talk about what he had experienced and seen in combat and began exploring with him how he could benefit from rehabilitation. She educated him about therapy. Without legs, he would not be able to walk independently, but there were options for greater independence that the therapist could offer. She also suggested regular meetings to review the potential for independent living and pursuing career opportunities.

Although this case example relates to an accident after military service, disabled veterans present unique problems. Due to America's recent wars there has been an increase in the number of soldiers who survive catastrophic injuries. Veterans who are double or triple amputees are not uncommon. Soldiers also suffer emotional trauma from seeing comrades severely injured or killed in horrific ways. Instances of brutality or even murder by traumatized military are all too common. Counseling is crucial to the healing process of the disabled and the traumatized, but challenging in a culture that demeans introspection and promotes a "stiff upper lip" response. Social workers with expertise with the military help soldiers address what has happened to them and help them develop coping mechanisms to move forward.

Case Example: A War Veteran with Survivor Guilt

The social worker at a veteran's hospital met with a new patient who was the only survivor of the battle his troop fought in Afghanistan. The patient had lost a leg in the battle. At the first meeting, the social worker took background information and asked the patient to talk about the battle where he lost his friends and his leg. The patient was reluctant to talk about it, explaining that he knew he was lucky to be alive. The social worker understood his reaction and suggested that he start attending a group with other men and women who had recently returned after sustaining injuries in battle. The social worker saw the group as a first step in allowing the patient to begin to articulate his fears in a group with others who have endured the same tragedies. Once the patient heard others talking about similar traumas, he could begin the process of looking at his losses and his guilt at surviving.

When helping a person who has newly acquired a disability, the social worker will spend more time listening to the person as he or she articulates feelings about the losses. This is especially significant when the disability is the result of an accident or the aftermath of a criminal assault. The social worker listens with a goal of helping the person identify and build on his /her coping skills and strengths.

Case Example: Helping a Rape Victim

A young woman was hospitalized after sustaining a fractured pelvis during an assault and rape. When the social worker met with her, the patient talked about her overwhelming fear, her terror of any male stranger, and how frightened she was that she may not be able to walk and was, therefore, more vulnerable. The social worker encouraged her to talk about what had happened to her, explaining that her many fears were valid. Over the course of several weeks they met regularly and the patient was able to describe in detail and articulate her fear of what had happened to her. As she began to receive rehabilitation (physical and occupational therapy) she became more distressed about her physical disabilities, but was still able to talk about what had happened and how her life had changed. The social worker also met with the patient's parents and encouraged them to seek help for themselves and to plan for what would happen after discharge. The social worker provided information on a community agency that could provide counseling for the patient and her parents. She also found an agency that supported rape victims with financial help.

Caregivers

Caregivers may be family members or paid attendants. Family members of chronically disabled people may have a network of supportive family and friends as well as people who can care for the disabled person when the primary caregiver needs relief. However, others may have limited support and limited resources. These caregivers may also benefit from social work counseling as well as help in accessing resources.

Case Example: Helping a Caregiver

The sister of a disabled woman met with the social worker at the day program the disabled woman attended. The sister's husband had had a stroke and was partially paralyzed. The client expressed her fear of having to be a

caregiver to two disabled people, as well as her sadness
about her husband's significant physical incapacity. The
social worker suggested that they plan to meet regularly for
a period of time so that they could talk over the client's
feelings of loss and fear. She also suggested that they could
look for resources in the community to assist the client with
home care.

Family members of those recently disabled may experience shock and anger at the loss of a functioning family member and need help in planning for the needs of the disabled person, as well as adapting to the changes in the family.

Case Example: Mediating Between a Nursing Home and a Family Member

The daughter of a new nursing home resident quickly
developed a reputation as a "complainer" among the staff.
The social worker met with the daughter and asked how
things were going. The daughter complained bitterly about
the poor care her mother received. She also demanded
reimbursement for the loss of cotton socks she had
purchased that had been "stolen." As they explored the
"poor care" and loss of socks, the social worker suggested

that perhaps the daughter was experiencing even greater losses. The daughter became very upset and began crying. She stated that her mother was driving her car only weeks ago and was now helpless and confused. The social worker suggested that she would work with the staff to be more responsive, with administration about reimbursement and she suggested they meet weekly to discuss the shock and grief she was experiencing since her mother's incapacitation. The social worker also encouraged the daughter to bring all problems and concerns to her and let her function as the point person with staff.

Paid attendants may have significant experience with the physical and emotional needs of people with disabilities, but beginning with a new patient or watching a person decline can be troubling to a caregiver. Social work intervention with an attendant may involve education about the client's emotional needs and what the attendant may anticipate when providing care.

Case Example: A Home Care Worker's Anxiety

A social worker from a home care agency received a complaint from the family member of an elderly woman about her home attendant. The social worker was surprised since the home attendant had been with this woman for a long time and there had been no previous complaints. The social worker met with the home attendant, who voiced concerns about the elderly woman's forgetfulness. She was worried about this change in the elderly woman's mental status. As they discussed her concern, it became clear that she was also worried about the woman's confused complaints to her family. The woman frequently called her son to complain that she hadn't eaten and was left all alone. The attendant was worried that she would lose her job. The social worker suggested that she might talk with the elderly woman about her fears, reminding her that she was there to help her. She also advised her to call the son and assure him that his mother was being cared for and that he could call her whenever he was worried about his mother. She arranged for a medical evaluation of the elderly woman to ascertain if there was a physical reason for her mental decline. She also suggested that she and the home attendant meet regularly for several weeks to make sure that the situation was stabilized.

Conclusion

These examples of social work services for people with disabilities illustrate the breath of social work interventions. Social workers are trained as counselors and listen and explore issues with the client to be certain that they understand the specifics of the problem. Counseling focuses on the strengths available to the client to work on the problems. The social worker also follows up, as needed, with the other people involved with the client, or, as indicated in the example above, encourages the client to reach out to a family member.

Knowledge of resources involves much more than making a referral. The social worker utilizes resources after ascertaining the needs of the client and the resources available. The social worker may have to talk to several agencies to find the right fit for the client, and may need to explore more than one resource to meet the client's needs.

The social worker also talks with others in managing a problem. In the example of the daughter of the nursing home resident, the social worker encouraged the daughter to bring her all problems and issues. This intervention was helpful to the daughter as well as the staff.

The social work model of practice truly reflects the importance of treating the whole person. The skills of the social worker include listening and understanding the "real" problems, assessing the needs of the client, working with others involved with the client, finding appropriate resources and providing follow up work with the client and the client's network.

Frances Brennan is a graduate of Columbia University School of Social Work. She has specialized in work with the elderly and the disabled. Ms. Brennan was the Director of Social Work at Mary Manning Walsh Home until her retirement in 2012. She is the co-author (with Ann Burack Weiss) of Gerontological Social Work Supervision (Haworth Press, 1991) and Gerontological Supervision: A Social Work Perspective (Routledge, 2008) as well as many articles on social work with the elderly. She is a member of the board of the Helen Rehr Center for Social Work Practice.

CHAPTER 10

SOCIAL WORK IN THE TERMINAL PHASE OF ILLNESS AND HOSPICE CARE

Elizabeth Alvarado, LCSW, ACHP-SW

Introduction

Hospice care is specialized compassionate care for terminally ill patients with a life expectancy of six months or less that focuses on caring, not curing, during the end of life. It can be delivered in different settings, and patients and families have a choice where and when the care is provided and who provides it.[6] A hospice program is one

---

[6] The term "hospice" can be traced back to medieval times, when it referred to a place of shelter and rest for weary or ill travelers on a long journey. Modern hospice care began in a suburb of London in 1948 when Dame Cicely Saunders founded St. Christopher's Hospice for terminally ill patients with a life expectancy of six months or less. Dame Saunders first introduced the idea of specialized care for the dying in the United States during a 1963 visit to Yale University.

that specializes in this end of life care, whether it is provided in the client's home, in a long-term care or nursing home facility, or in a hospital hospice unit.

Social Workers in Hospice Care

Social workers are part of the core team of a hospice program, which also consists of physicians, nurses, clergy, and others who interact with patients and families dealing with a terminally ill patient. Wherever the care is provided, the social worker's first responsibility is to evaluate the needs of the patient and the family. The social worker completes a visit – at home, in the hospital, or in a nursing home -- and talks with the patient, the family, and the caregivers involved to identify emotional, psychological, social, financial, and physical needs.

A critically important skill of the social worker is to establish a trusting and open working relationship with the new patient and the family and help to communicate important pieces of information about them to other hospice caregivers so they can understand and work successfully with them. Understanding the family dynamics surrounding the patient is a core social work skill. Social workers are aware that when facing terminal illness, families often struggle with many emotions. It may be difficult for some patients or family members to choose the holistic comfort of hospice, particularly since ours is a death-defying society, and many opt for active treatment during the very end stage of illness. Family members may disagree with each other on the end of life decisions of their loved one. In these cases, the social worker can help educate family members regarding any misconceptions or dilemmas they may be facing during this stressful time.

Most families are exhausted or anxious adjusting to the reality that a family member or friend is dying. Social workers can help them talk about what is most important and offer options to support the decision to have the person die at home versus in a facility. Ethical dilemmas, such as whether to withdraw or withhold treatment, may also arise, and social workers are adept at problem solving, advocacy, and facilitating the proper resources to find solutions that are helpful for each family. Financial concerns may also be an issue at the end of life, and this is another area where social workers are extremely knowledgeable and successful at helping people navigate resources such as health insurance coverage, medical costs, bills, or accessing disability income.

Hospice social workers have skills and competencies that help to create a safe place for patients and their families to begin the dialogue about preparing for death, which is an important part of the hospice journey. It is the social worker's role to facilitate this "safe place" and help people accept or adjust to the pending death of their loved one. Psychological/spiritual stressors such as anxiety, guilt, or depression can be addressed and managed through counseling (including emotional support), education, or short-term psychological techniques. For those patients or family members experiencing tremendous emotional grief, the social worker may act as a grief counselor or hospice therapist. In some cases where there is a need for additional psychological counseling, the social worker will put the patient or family member in touch with a licensed therapist.

While the hospice nurse's role is to present information about the physical needs of the newly admitted patient, the social worker's role is to present his/her psycho-social needs assessment to help educate the other team members about issues such as:

- Who is this person?

- What kind of work did he or she do?

- How does this terminal illness affect the person?

- How is the patient coping with the terminal illness?

- Is there a suicide risk?

- Who is the primary decision maker?

- What is the best way to reach that person?

- How is the family coping?

- Does the patient have a good family support system?

- Does the patient or the family have financial concerns?

- What additional help is needed in the home?

- What resources are needed?

- What is the preferred communication system?

- Are the patient and family open to the idea of talking with a spiritual care counselor or a volunteer?

Social workers help to bring forward important information from their initial psychosocial assessment about the individual's cultural or religious ideals regarding the end of life process that need to be acknowledged and respected as well.

Another important role for the social worker is to assess the risk of suicide in every patient and family. Uncontrolled pain has been recognized as an important contributing factor to suicide in cancer and AIDS patients. Older patients seem to be particularly vulnerable. The social worker will use a suicide risk assessment tool to assess and monitor the situation and make sure that if a patient or family member is at risk, they are given the proper attention and intervention.

Hospice Care at Home

A book by Dr. Elisabeth Kubler-Ross entitled *On Death and Dying* identified the five stages that patients described during the process of dying: denial and isolation, anger, bargaining, depression, and acceptance. In the book, Dr. Kubler-Ross made a plea for care delivered in the home, called Home Hospice Care, as opposed to treatment in an institutional setting like a nursing home, and argued that patients should have a choice and the ability to participate in the decisions that affect their destiny. Hospice Home Care is covered under Medicare, Medicaid, and most private insurance plans. Patients can receive hospice care regardless of their ability to pay (people who are uninsured or underinsured may receive what is known as charity care).

When hospice care is delivered in the home setting, it is by a team of professionals that includes doctors, nurses, social workers, counselors, home health aides, clergy, therapists, and trained volunteers. The hospice care team will evaluate a patient's physical condition when first admitted to the program, assessing the pain and symptoms. Any discomfort, pain, or side effects from medications will be addressed immediately. The primary goal is to make sure that is the patient is as free of pain and symptoms as possible, yet still alert enough to enjoy the people around him or her and make important decisions. Each of these individual professional team members offers the patient and the family expert knowledge and support during the terminal phase of the illness. Palliative care is holistic care focused on pain, symptoms, and social, emotional and spiritual needs, and like hospice care, it is not focused on cure but on enhancing the quality of life until death.

Since people differ in their spiritual needs and religious beliefs, spiritual care may be set up to meet the specific needs of the patient or family members. It may include helping the patient look at what death means to him/her, helping him/her say good-bye, or helping with a certain religious ceremony or ritual. Spiritual care can mean re-examining beliefs, exploring beliefs of an afterlife, reconciling life choices, examining loving relationships or relationships that were painful, discovering meaning, prayer, and meditation or discovering the meaning of the person's life.

Respite Care

While someone is receiving hospice services at home, family and caregivers may need some time away from the patient and the strain of caretaking. The hospice benefit service offers them a break through respite care, which is offered for a five-day period. During this time, the patient will be cared for either in the hospice facility or in beds that are set aside for this in nursing homes or hospitals. Families can plan a mini-vacation, go to special events, or simply get much-needed rest at home while the patient is cared for in an inpatient setting. Family members may feel guilty about taking time off away from their loved one. The social worker can help them realize that they need to first take care of themselves so that they can be healthy, strong, and able to then care for their loved one. Dealing with the intense emotions associated with grief can be overwhelming without the proper support and information. Social workers have information and skills that help facilitate grief and help people avoid obstacles that can lead to more complicated reactions like depression.

Bereavement

Bereavement is the time of mourning after a loss. The hospice care team works with surviving loved ones to help them through the grieving process. A social worker, clergy member, or trained volunteer or counselor provides support to survivors through visits, phone calls, and/or letter contact, as well as through support groups. The hospice team can refer family members and care-giving friends to other medical or professional care, if needed.

Bereavement counseling means emotional, psychosocial and spiritual support and services that are provided before or after the death of the patient to assist with issues related to grief, loss, and adjustment. Bereavement counseling is available to caregivers and families for thirteen months after the death of a loved one.

Volunteers

Hospice volunteers play an important role in hospice care in the United States. Medicare Conditions of Participation require that volunteers provide at least 5% of total patient care hours in hospice care. Hospice services are unique in this respect. Volunteers have three main functions in a hospice care program. They include spending time with patients and families, providing clerical support, and helping provide other supports.

Case Example: Assessing the Best Option for the Patient and Her Family

Ms. Z was a 60-year-old widowed woman with a diagnosis of brain cancer, who prior to being admitted to a hospice program had received several rounds of chemotherapy and multiple surgeries to remove a brain tumor that kept coming back. The brain cancer continued to spread to various parts of her brain despite continuous treatment.

Her primary physician referred her to hospice when she reached a life expectancy of 6 months or less.

The hospice program was called in immediately. The admission nurse made arrangements to visit the home and meet with Ms. Z and her two adult daughters. The admission nurse educated them about the hospice program and obtained signed consent forms for admission to the program.

One of the daughters lived with Ms. Z and was the health care proxy. (A health care proxy is a document, typically state regulated, which allows a person to designate someone to make health care decisions for another in the event of incapacity.) However, Mrs. Z.'s daughter worked fulltime and could not take time off to care for her mother. Ms. Z, who was confused, could not sign a DNR (Do Not Resuscitate order) because she was unable to understand what she would be signing. The daughters needed more time to think about signing an advance directive for their mom.

An advance directive is a document that allows a person (or his or her proxy) to specify the medical care the person should receive in the event of incapacitation. It is a social worker's role to educate about the different types of advance directives and assist the patient and family in completing one if needed.

The social worker prepared for a visit with Ms. Z and her two daughters by reviewing the notes completed by the admission nurse. The social worker scheduled a home visit with the family to gather information and complete an assessment of the current needs and goals of care.

At the assessment meeting, the daughters expressed an interest in pursuing skilled nursing home placement for their mother. The daughters reported they were limited in the number of days and hours they could provide care and supervision in the home because of their own jobs and family responsibilities. Both daughters became extremely tearful as they shared with the social worker the mother's terminal illness and now the decision for hospice care instead of active treatment.

The two daughters reported guilty feelings about placing their mother in a nursing home. Often family members experience guilt or feel like they are abandoning their loved one when they consider this option. The social worker is able to help assess caregiver stress and emotional turmoil and provide supportive counseling to the family. Social workers use their clinical counseling skills to create a safe space for family members to begin important discussions about how they feel about taking care of the loved one at home on the hospice program.

The social worker in Ms. Z's case reviewed the skilled nursing home placement application process with Ms. Z's daughters, along with the necessary steps, including the paperwork needed by the nursing home for a review. It is the social worker's role to gather the forms needed and send them to the admission offices of the chosen nursing homes. The social worker is responsible for calling the skilled nursing homes and learning if a decision has been made and communicating back to the patient and family as needed. Once a bed is offered by a facility and the patient or family agrees, the social worker will help make the necessary arrangements for the move into the skilled nursing home.

The hospice social worker was able to assess the emotional needs of both the patient and family, provide new

information, educate about advance directives, provide
supportive counseling, and assist with skilled nursing home
placement. The daughters were pleased when Ms. Z was
approved at a nursing home nearby which they could visit
often. The same team of hospice professionals visited Ms. Z
in the skilled nursing home and she died peacefully with
compassionate and comforting care.

Hospice in a Long-Term Care/Nursing Home Facility

Many hospice care agencies have contracted beds in skilled nursing facilities. As the average life span in the United States has increased, so has the number of individuals who die of chronic progressive diseases that require longer and more sustained care. An increasing number of these individuals reside in nursing homes prior to their death. This rise has been mirrored by growth in the number of hospice patients who reside in nursing homes.

Choosing the right skilled nursing home is not an easy decision for patients and families to make. The social worker can help by providing them with a list of those facilities closest to home or the facilities that are contracted with the same hospice agency. If the patient's application is medically and financially accepted, it means the patient can be admitted to the skilled nursing home and continue to receive hospice care from the same hospice team (doctor, nurses, social workers, home health aides, volunteers and spiritual care counselors) that was visiting him or her at home; only now the setting has changed to visits in the skilled nursing home.

After a person is admitted into the skilled nursing home, a care plan meeting is scheduled with the skilled nursing home team and the hospice social worker and nurse to make sure everyone is on the same page concerning the goals of care. At this care plan meeting, it is recommended that family and caregivers are present to help communicate any special needs for the patient. Assistance with advance care planning to ensure that all treatments meet the wishes of the person receiving care is also within the purview of social work intervention. Advance care planning entails making decisions about treatment in end of care and funeral planning, and communicating this with loved ones and in a will or other legal documents.

Hospice Care in a Hospital

An admission to an inpatient unit is usually for a newly diagnosed hospital patient with a terminal diagnosis or a current hospice home care recipient whose pain and symptoms are not being well managed in the home and who requires a change in medication or other specialized treatment to minimize the pain and suffering. It is important for the patient and family to maintain ongoing communication with the hospice program about any changes in the patient that may require a trip to the hospital. The hospice nurse will arrange for inpatient care and will stay involved in the care and with the family. The patient can go back to in-home care when he or she and family members are ready. Once admitted to an inpatient setting, the hospice social worker will work with the patient and the team to determine post-hospital discharge planning when the patient is medically stable for discharge home.

Conclusion

Here are some of the ways the social worker can help once a patient is referred to a hospice program: (1) help facilitate decision making about medical care and plans; (2) help family members adapt to role changes brought on by the illness and improve family communication; (3) help manage difficult feelings such as anxiety, depression, fear, confusion, anger, and grief; (4) help arrange adequate home, hospital or nursing home care; (5) help provide information about community resources; and (6) help resolve financial strain through access to legal entitlements and benefits.

Sometimes it is just the presence of the social worker that offers a sense of comfort and support to the patient and family, because they know the social worker is there to help.

Hospice social workers thus bring a complex set of unique skills to individuals and families struggling with one of life's most challenging and painful experiences. Using the assessment, diagnosis, and intervention skills that are the hallmark of social work education and practice, the social worker's approach is a holistic one. It takes into consideration not only the patient's medical, emotional and financial needs, but those of the patient's family. Those skills are the glue that bind together all of the patient's needs together in the effort to minimize suffering, reduce family tension, and ease the patient's remaining months of life for all concerned.

Elizabeth Alvarado is a Licensed Clinical Social Worker with 20 years of clinical practice working with individuals, families, and groups. She has provided clinical supervision and administrative oversight to community based programs serving the homebound elderly, caregivers, people with mental health disorders, and the chronically medically ill. She taught at Columbia School of Social Work and is currently adjunct professor at the Graduate School of Social Work at Hunter College and Boston University. She is on the Board of the Helen Rehr Center for Social Work Practice and does private consulting work in New York.

CHAPTER 11

SOCIAL WORKERS WHO ARE CARE MANAGERS

Leonie Nowitz, LCSW, B.C.D.

Introduction

Care managers are professionally trained social workers, licensed or certified, who handle the full spectrum of tasks required to develop and implement care plans for those in need of specialized assistance. The clients are typically those who are frail elderly and/or disabled. Many care managers are private practitioners paid by insurance policies or client funds. Some social work agencies also provide care management on a sliding scale with philanthropic support to those who cannot afford to pay for care managers. Many care managers are also trained in family therapy, which is extremely helpful in dealing with conflicts among family members which frequently arise in such cases.

The care manager is responsible for assessing the needs of the client, the availability of relatives or friends to assist in the client's care, how those caregivers relate to the client and each other, the client's access to insurance or private funds to pay for care, and the types of specialized services that may suit the client's needs. The care manager assists the person and his or her care networks to develop a viable care plan, and provides information to them about resources that would best enable the person to maintain or improve his/her functioning. When necessary, a care manager monitors the care, assists the client to obtain government entitlements, and, where appropriate, finds alternative living arrangements such as adult homes or nursing homes.

Assessment of the Client

The care manager focuses on the following information in assessing a client's situation:

1. Health status and current illnesses/ disabilities that affect functional capacities. In addition to assessing the cognitive and physical capacities of the person, the care manager assesses which of those can be improved.

2. Response to changes in health. Is the person depressed or withdrawn? If cognitively impaired, is he/she denying any problem and continuing activities that are unsafe?

3. Impact of illness on social activities. Has the illness/disability affected the person's socialization? What resources are still available? What new situations would be of interest?

4. View of the current support system. Is it difficult for the person to ask family or friends for help? Is this person satisfied with the current caregivers? What would he or she like to be different?

5. Financial resources. Is the client willing or able to pay for services? Should legal consultation be considered to plan for long-term care and assess the

person's eligibility for entitlements, such as Medicaid home care? Questions about the person's and the family's views about accepting entitlements should be raised.

6. Housing needs. The care manager needs to evaluate the living environment and determine whether adjustments can be made to accommodate the situation or whether it might be better to consider a change in residence. While safety and care needs are supreme, the person's values regarding where he or she lives need to be respected.

7. Information from the formal outside systems. Information from the caregivers broadens the care manager's understanding. With permission from the person and family, the care manager listens to the physicians, nurses, physical therapists, home care workers, housekeepers – that is, all those involved and interested in the care situation.

Assessment of the Family Members and Other Caregivers

Illness and changed functioning evoke strong reactions in older and/or disabled persons and those close to them. Many aged/disabled men and women feel diminished and find it difficult to ask for assistance. Family members who assume care-giving tasks can have mixed emotions: wanting to provide the care, yet feeling overburdened by the conflicting demands on their time, their work, and their other family members. As the care manager gets more information, he/she can develop a care plan that distributes care-giving tasks and enables the family and formal systems, such as outside agencies and providers, to work together.

To best serve the client, the care manager must evaluate the family's response to the situation by exploring various questions. Are family members involved in the client's care? If so, in what ways? What are their long-term plans? Are there conflicts or disagreement among family members? Care managers need to understand the lifetime history of how the family members relate to and care for each other. For example, if an elderly spouse is providing all of the care to her husband with dementia, the care manager needs to understand whether she has difficulty asking family members for help. Has she always been the primary caregiver? Have others in the family provided care in the past, and to whom?

Because families traditionally assume care-giving tasks, the social worker will include all those in the care-giving system in the initial meeting with the client. If family members live far away, the care manager will arrange to talk with them on the telephone. It is important to ask about family members whom the original callers may not want to include and perhaps seek out their points of view and give them opportunities to offer assistance. Including all family members is often the best option for the patient and the family. It spreads the responsibilities among the family members and encourages them to collaborate rather than engage in disruptive conflict.

A care manager can help families consider new possibilities of working together. If a family resists inviting significant family members into the process, the care manager helps them consider the consequences, such as the excluded party working against their care plan, and possibly moving against the best interests of their relative. The social worker needs to provide family and friends with information about care or services that are consistent with their needs and values.

The care manager can offer counseling individually or to appropriate family members to help air differences and develop better understanding and collaboration. The social worker assesses caregiver stress and can help the family members consider resources within the family or outside of it. For example, counseling is important in helping family members understand how changes in health can affect the client's behavior and how they might better respond to them. The social worker needs to be sensitive to every member's pain and discomfort around the health problems and changed relationships. The caring and values transmitted from one family member to another can leave a legacy to future generations.

Case Example: Addressing Family Conflicts

Two adult children were concerned about their ill parents. Although reluctant to invite their sister to the initial

meeting because of her conflicts with their parents, they
included her, at the care manager's suggestion, to give her
the opportunity to participate in developing a care plan.
This sister flew in from California, acknowledged her
differences with her parents with the care manager's help,
but showed her concern. The care manager also advised
the two adult children that it was important to acknowledge
what the California sister was doing and to involve her in
the plan they were developing, since they and their parents
could use her help.

Assessment of the Willingness of the Client or the Family to Accept Outside Services

After evaluating the resources in the family system, the
social worker needs to assess the gaps in care and what
services the family would consider to balance their care
giving. Assessment of the patient-kin network is an
ongoing process. As the person's needs change, the care
plans change. The social worker looks at everyone in the
system and considers his or her perspectives. This includes
the client, the patient-kin network, and the outside systems
and professionals, such as someone with the client's power

of attorney, accountants, physicians, nurses, home care attendants, and agency personnel.

It is difficult for many older or disabled persons and their families to accept care from strangers. Cultural beliefs and multigenerational patterns of family care giving can affect their acceptance of help from home care to day care, respite services, community centers, or alternate housing. The social worker needs to assess any client or family's unwillingness to accept help. What is behind an older/disabled person's rejection of a paid caregiver or Medicaid home worker? Does he or she regard such aid as expensive, shameful, intrusive, or a denial of his or her autonomy? What are the viewpoints of all family members?

The social worker needs to understand the concerns and fears of older/disabled persons who refuse care that would secure their safety and well-being. Ongoing counseling, trust, and relationship building between the care manager, the person and the family may generally encourage acceptance of care. A resourceful care manager may be able to find the kind of person with whom the client would be most comfortable, allowing the client to interview potential candidates with congruent personality and skills.

This might give the person the impetus to consider the home care worker.

Case Example: A Wife's Determination to Do it all Herself

A wife in her eighties would not allow herself a moment's respite from caring for her husband, who had severe dementia. Despite ongoing counseling, she could only allow herself "a break" when she was hospitalized for a heart attack. With the social worker's help, she gradually realized that she could not continue to care for him in this manner and applied to a multi-care facility where he moved into the nursing home and she into the adjacent residence.

When family members have difficulty taking responsibility for relatives, particularly those who are cognitively impaired, the care manager needs to assess their difficulties and guide them into appropriate roles. This process involves reaching out to them, relating safety and care concerns, and listening to them. If these efforts fail and the client is at serious risk, the care manager needs to help the family consider a guardianship proceeding and the possibility of working with protective services. When family members have divergent views on the best care options, the care manager needs to consider their points of view and sources of stress, continuing to search for the solutions that will best fit the older person's needs.

Case Example: Disagreement among Siblings

Holly, a social worker/care manager for Mrs. Newman, called a family meeting with her client's daughter and two sons. Mrs. Newman's cognitive status was declining significantly and she was having difficulty keeping her helpers. The sons felt it was time to consider a nursing home. The daughter was opposed to placement. Holly suggested they consider both options. She would arrange for visits to a few homes. She also suggested an agency that specialized in home care for the cognitively impaired. They could see how well she could be managed at home while considering the option for nursing home placement.

Ongoing Needs

Some families find the initial consultation and care plan sufficient to guide them. Other families consult on an intermittent basis to clarify concerns and consider alternate options for care. Still other families engage the care manager in some of the tasks, such as accessing home care services, monitoring their parent's care or applying for entitlements. Care managers are sensitive to the specific needs of each family and offer help to a family in stress.

Conclusion

The social worker/care manager needs to be knowledgeable about the impact of long-term disabilities on older/disabled people and their families. Good assessment skills are essential to understanding the challenges faced by the person and family members. In addition to assessing needs and services, the care manager needs to be sensitive to the values of the family, and introduce care in a way that will make it understandable and easier to accept. The care manager's knowledge of resources and connections to specialists, home care personnel, community agencies, entitlement programs and support groups will help the person and family gain access to the specialists and programs that best will serve them. The care manager's ability to understand how each family system works, in order to guide families to more collaborative efforts that include the formal system, is critical in helping ease the stress for all.

Leonie Nowitz, LCSW has worked in the field of aging for 40 years. After graduating from the Columbia School of Social Work, she became a social worker at the Jewish Home and Hospital for the Aged. She received her Post-Masters Certificate in Advanced Social Work, specializing in Family Therapy, from Hunter College School of Social Work. She founded her professional private, service organization, The Center for Lifelong Growth, which provides comprehensive case management for the elderly, the disabled and their families. Ms. Nowitz is a Founding Member of the National Association of Professional Geriatric Care Managers.

CHAPTER 12

SOCIAL WORK SERVICES IN LONG-TERM CARE

Frances Brennan, LCSW

Introduction

People enter long-term care facilities – commonly called nursing homes -- due to one of several kinds of changes in their health. An elderly person may experience a decline in her ability to care for herself. A son may see his father as increasingly disheveled and unable to bathe, shave or dress appropriately. A trusted aide may determine that she can no longer provide the level of care her patient needs. The person (disabled, elderly, or both) and close relatives or friends may begin a process of looking for and applying to one or more long-term care facilities.

In other circumstances, people who have had a significant medical event (a stroke, a bad fall, or major surgery, for example) may be referred to a nursing facility that provides rehabilitation. These facilities have dedicated short stay units where patients receive post-hospital care including physical, occupational, and speech therapy. Typically, patients leaving the hospital will be advised by staff about the benefits of rehabilitation in a nursing facility (commonly called sub-acute rehabilitation) and will likely be quickly transferred when a facility has an available bed.

The third reason is for hospice care -- comfort care for people with a terminal illness, which is described in Chapter 10. Many nursing facilities contract with hospice programs and may offer hospice care for those at the end of life. Hospice patients may stay in the facility receiving care until the end of life. Others may stabilize or benefit from rehabilitation and return home with hospice care.

Social workers play a very important role in the lives of long term, short stay, and hospice patients.

Long-Term Care

Long-term placement is a major and traumatic life transition for the new patient and his or her family members and friends. New patients and/or their caregivers and families typically have difficulty understanding how the institution works and how to get their needs met. While nurses and physicians handle the patient's medical care, the social worker in long-term care is typically responsible for the non-medical needs of the patients and their families. This includes an initial needs assessment developed through an interview with the patient and/or family. Interventions may include counseling both the new patient and family about the impact of this major life change, interpreting the needs of the new patient to other staff, helping the patient/family understand the complex systems of the institution, and advocating for patients and families who cannot or have been unsuccessful in advocating on their own.

In most facilities a new patient will share a room and have only limited space and storage. While the goal of most facilities is to provide a home-like environment, the medical model, which focuses on the health of the person, remains the norm in most institutional settings. But it is equally important that the facility makes the resident's needs a priority and the social worker plays a critical role in ensuring that happens.

Case Example: Calming an Angry, Defiant New Patient

The social worker at Mayfield Nursing Home checked on Mrs. Hart, who had been admitted to the home the day before. She found her yelling at her daughter that she wanted to pack her bags immediately and return home. "I don't care if I fall and die!!" Her daughter was crying and distraught. The social worker asked Mrs. Hart to sit down for a moment. She explained that a nursing home is not a prison and no one has to stay against her will. She further explained that it would be her job to work out a plan to discharge Mrs. Hart if she was unhappy. She also suggested that this major life transition was upsetting and Mrs. Hart needed to think about the reasons she decided to enter the facility. Mrs. Hart became calmer. The social worker asked her to give the home a trial, attend a few of the programs, and see how she felt in a few days. She offered to check with Mrs. Hart daily and she reminded Mrs. Hart that the social worker would be available at any time. Reiterating that Mrs. Hart had options, she suggested to Mrs. Hart's daughter that she and her mother spend a little time in the garden.

In this example, the social worker anticipated that a new patient would have a significant reaction to admission. She presented the patient with alternatives, but reinforced the reality of her care needs.

Social workers in long-term care also work with patients and their families over time. Common problems include conflict between patients sharing rooms or public spaces, changes in medical conditions (which may necessitate relocation to a different unit), and problems getting concrete needs met. Most nursing homes have patient councils or other groups to address concerns or complaints. Typically, a social worker leads or participates in these meetings.

Short-Term Rehabilitation

Social workers on rehabilitation units provide the same services as are offered in long-term care, but typically admission into the facility is not as traumatic for a short-term stay. Rather, admission is perceived as a major step toward recovery. On rehabilitation units, social workers are more likely to be discharge planners.

Discharge planning also involves an initial psychosocial assessment, which will identify the person's strengths and weaknesses, family and community supports and resources available to the person returning to the community. The discharge plan can be easy if the patient has community supports and a safe living arrangement. However, it can be very difficult if there are problems in the home (for example, stairs, bathrooms that cannot accommodate wheelchairs, disorganization and clutter) limited resources, or if the patient denies the need for hands-on care at home. The social worker provides skilled intervention to work on these problems. Problems at home may require engaging the family or friends in making the home safe and livable. If there is no family, the social worker must find community resources to work with the patient, as well as help the patient understand what has to be done to return home safely.

Case Example: Finding Resources for a Patient Who Wants to Leave

Mr. Connor, an 81-year-old gentleman, was admitted to a sub-acute unit after hospitalization for dehydration. He also had a diagnosis of personality disorder. He received occupational therapy for seven days, but had minimal rehabilitation needs. He wanted to return home. Mr. Connor had no known family or friends and advised the social worker that it was not her business to worry about help at home. As the social worker anticipated, he was not approved for home care services under Medicare by the vendor commonly used in the facility. Mr. Connor did inform the social worker that he ate two meals a day at a senior center near his home. She called the center and spoke to the social worker there who knew him and said she would work with him more closely on his return. She also called the Medicare vendor who agreed to reassess him now that a new plan was in place. She spoke again to Mr. Connor and explained that the home care services

were covered under Medicare, and the staff felt he would
benefit from some rehabilitation and nursing follow up at
home. He did agree, with the understanding that he would
decide when the services ended.

In this example, the social worker had to persuade the client to accept services, as well as persuade the vendor agency to provide them. The fact that he enjoyed the meals at the senior center was a significant element in putting the rest of the plan in place. The social worker also respected this man's independence and determination and worked with his strengths rather than his diagnosis.

Patients who deny they need help can challenge the most experienced social worker. Counseling that includes encouraging the patient by explaining that people often get stronger and more independent over time is often successful. Using other staff, family members, or outside resources are often helpful in encouraging a patient to allow services at home.

Ultimately, the agency and the social worker must have a safe discharge plan before a short stay patient can return to the community. At the same time, unless a person is severely mentally ill or has a pronounced dementia, he/or she is an adult and can make a bad decision. If a patient insists on leaving without appropriate care or to an unsafe home, the social worker will contact the local agency that follows up on adults in need of protection. It is not uncommon for a patient to comply with appropriate home care arrangements rather than have a governmental agency come into their lives.

Long-Term Care and Financial Resources

Limited financial resources present a series of other problems for some patients. Even patients with sufficient resources anticipate that the government or private insurance will cover all or most of the services of a short stay program. It is typically the social worker who explains the limits of government and other insurances and helps the patient understand what has to be supplemented with private resources. Patients with little or no personal financial resources need the social worker's help exploring what, if any, additional supports can be accessed. Sadly, some patients remain in facilities longer than they need because their insurance or government benefits may only cover care in a nursing home, but not at home.

Hospice

Social workers in hospice settings work closely with the patient, family, and other team members. The goal is always the comfort and support for the dying patient and his or her family and friends. Hospice social workers focus on the quality of the time left as well as acknowledging the fears and anger associated with the dying process. Sometimes the social worker is the primary counselor to the patient; sometimes their role is with the family or friends. Usually, the interdisciplinary team determines the best treatment plan with the patient and family/friends.

Case Example: Working with Conflicts within the Family

The social worker on the hospice unit at Chestnut Lodge Nursing Home greeted a new patient and his son. The new patient, Mr. Rice, introduced his son and also said his wife would be along shortly. When the physician came in to see Mr. Rice, the son asked to speak to the social worker. The son advised that Mr. Rice had been married for 35 years in a second marriage after a bitter divorce from the son's mother. The son and his sister did not speak to their stepmother. He was certain that the hospice care was her idea and said that he and his sister believed that their father should have more medical treatment. He also said that his father would always placate his wife, as he does not like confrontation. Later the social worker met the wife who appeared appropriately saddened by her husband's condition. The social worker then consulted with the physician and the psychiatrist.

A review of Mr. Rice's medical condition indicated that hospice was appropriate for this patient and that further treatment would be painful and futile. The psychiatrist evaluated Mr. Rice and determined that he had decision-making capacity. The social worker then spoke to Mr. Rice privately and asked how he had decided on hospice. Mr. Rice talked at length about his life and his family. He expressed regret over the circumstances of his divorce and the impact it had on his children. He spoke of his love for his children and for his wife as well as his realization that there was no treatment to help him. He said he wished his medical condition was not fatal, but understood that it was. He hoped that in the time he had left, he could comfort and be comforted by his wife and children, but also knew that the time they spent with him would have to be separate.

The social worker asked what Mr. Rice needed from him. Mr. Rice asked that he help his children let him go.

In this example, the social worker gathered a significant amount of information from three of the four parties involved. He then consulted with his team to ascertain Mr. Rice's physical and mental status. With this information, he determined how he would proceed to assist this family. The social worker's role in this family system would be working with the son and daughter to help them understand and respect their father's wishes.

Conclusion

Voluntary, not for profit-nursing facilities have trained qualified social workers. Those seeking a nursing facility for long term care, short term rehabilitation or hospice should consider the benefits derived from having a skilled social worker as a part of the care team to assist the resident and family with adjustment, advocacy and personal problems.

Frances Brennan is a graduate of Columbia School of Social Work. She has specialized in work with the elderly and the disabled. Ms. Brennan was the Director of Social Work at Mary Manning Walsh Home until her retirement in 2012. She is the co-author (with Ann Burack Weiss) of Gerontological Social Work Supervision *(Haworth, 1991) and* Gerontological Supervision: A Social Work Perspective *(Routledge, 2008) as well as many articles on social work with the elderly. She is a member of board of the Helen Rehr Center for Social Work Practice.*

CHAPTER 13

SOCIAL WORK IN A HOSPITAL EMERGENCY ROOM

Carole Friedler, LCSW

Introduction

Social workers who are service providers in Hospital Emergency Departments (ERs) are specially trained to help patients and their families with the anxiety, stress, and fear they may experience while seeking emergency care. This can be caused by the symptoms that led to the ER visit, the wait to be assigned a room, and/or to see a doctor, or the intensity of the atmosphere in a busy ER. Added to this may be a patient's confusion and uncertainty about her/his diagnosis and how it will be handled.

Patients come to the ER for a myriad of reasons, including, but not limited to, illness, child or adult abuse, domestic violence, homelessness, psychiatric crises, financial assistance, and sexual assault. A patient's medical crisis can be due to an accident (i.e. a car crash or a fall), or related to the sudden onset of illness (i.e. a stroke or heart attack). In some hospitals, patients are assessed for social work intervention at the time of ER admission. In others, the social workers are contacted by the medical team on an as-needed basis. In either case, the social worker helps the patient and his or her family understand how the ER functions and how to interpret the information communicated to them. In some cases, the patient or family needs a language interpreter as well. The social worker can also help the patient and family sort out the options for care, and can provide support throughout the visit and sometimes even afterwards.

The social worker's tasks can include the following:
- Assesses the ability of the patient and/or the family to give and receive medical information.
- Assists in helping to calm the patient and family; when necessary, acts as an intermediary with the medical team to facilitate communication.
- Contacts the patient's family (if the patient is alone and so wishes).

- Helps the patient and family to obtain necessary information in order to make decisions about medical care.
- Discusses advanced directives (health care proxy information, living wills, etc.) when appropriate.
- Educates the patient and family about Emergency Department protocols in order to lessen their fears and anxiety.
- Advocates for the patient/family's needs such as obtaining information, and providing support and referrals to outside services.

Case Example: Providing Information, Clarification, and Reassurance

A 55-year-old male was brought to the Emergency Room by ambulance after calling 911. He was at work when he began to experience some chest pain, and became cold, sweaty, and nauseous. His co-workers called 911, and he was transported to the hospital. On arrival, the Emergency Medical Service reported on the events leading up to patient's Emergency Room transport. The patient was evaluated immediately by a triage nurse (who determines which patients are in danger and must be seen first). Vital signs, EKG, and blood work were done. The social worker was then able to talk with the patient, who appeared pale, anxious, and worried. He responded to questions about his family situation: he was married with two teenage children. His wife did not work, and he was able to give her cell phone number to the social worker, who obtained his consent to call her. Although he worked as a lawyer in the city, the family lived in the suburbs.

The team from the Cardiac Catheterization Unit came to see the patient to evaluate him for treatment. While they were talking with the patient, the social worker called the patient's wife and told her that her husband had been brought to the Emergency Room from his office. When the treating physician was available, she spoke to the patient's wife to explain the current medical situation. She told her that it was likely that the patient had suffered a heart attack, and would be taken shortly to the Catheterization Lab to have stents placed. The social worker then spoke again with the patient's wife, who was understandably quite upset. The social worker provided support to the wife and informed her how to get to the Emergency Department. The social worker offered to wait for the wife and escort her to the Catheterization Lab. The wife arranged for her neighbor to talk with the children when they arrived home from school and called her sister to ask her to drive to the city with her.

The social worker then gave all of that information to the patient, who was relieved to hear that his wife would be coming, and that she would not be driving alone. The social worker explained that she would bring his wife to the unit where the patient would be and that she would be able to talk with the doctors there, when the procedure was finished. About an hour and a half later, the wife arrived at the Emergency Department and was met by the social worker. She was quite frantic and desperate to find out about her husband's condition. The social worker took the wife to the Catheterization Lab waiting area. She alerted the staff to the wife's arrival, and waited with her and her sister, until a nurse from the lab came to talk with her about her husband's current condition. She explained that the procedure was almost finished and her husband was doing well. His wife would be able to see him shortly and the physician would come out to talk with her in a few minutes. The wife was greatly relieved, and appeared much calmer. She and her sister waited for the arrival of the physician in the waiting area.

The social worker alerted the unit social worker in the department where the patient would be transferred after the procedure about the events leading up to this procedure, so that there would be ongoing support for the patient and his wife.

The Social Worker's Role in Discharge Planning

The social worker's role also involves developing a safe and appropriate discharge plan in cases where it is important that the patient be linked with medical and other community supports that will promote optimal health and stability after leaving the hospital. The social worker has to address the following issues prior to discharge:

- Can the patient return home? Is there anyone else at home?

- Did the patient have any home care services prior to the Emergency Room visit? Is there any ongoing nursing or medical care required for discharge?
- Will the patient need home care nursing? A physical therapist? Laboratory work? Equipment such as a walker, hospital bed, or bathroom equipment?
- Will the patient be able to function at the same level as when he/she came in to the Emergency Room? Was this sufficient?
- Will the patient require the help of another person? How many hours are required and what are the tasks with which the patient requires assistance?
- Is the patient able to afford the necessary medical or home care? What insurance, if any, might cover those services?

Case Example: Offering Support and Concrete Services

The patient was an 85-year-old woman who was brought to the Emergency Room by ambulance unable to walk. The ambulance report stated that she fell at home the previous night while going to the bathroom, and remained on the

*floor until this morning, when she did not come to the door
when her aide arrived.*

*The social worker spoke with the ambulance drivers and
learned that the patient lives in a one-bedroom apartment
in a high rise building. The apartment appeared orderly,
but with a lot of furniture and small rugs. The social
worker met with the patient at her bedside, together with
her aide, who had accompanied her to the Emergency
Room and remained with her. The patient was in obvious
pain. She was able to give the following history. She lived
alone, is a widow, and has two children, both of whom live
out of town and are married. She is in touch with both of
them, and they come to see her when they are able. Her
daughter lives in New Jersey with her husband, and her son
is in Florida with his wife. She had not contacted them yet.
In discussion with the Emergency Department physician,
the social worker learned that the patient appeared to have
a fractured hip. She was sent for X-rays and the diagnosis
was confirmed.*

*While waiting for consultation with the orthopedic surgeon,
the social worker returned to the patient to continue to find
out more about her situation and to provide emotional*

support. The social worker offered to assist the patient to contact her family, as the patient realized she must do. She did not want to upset her daughter, but knew that her daughter, who usually called in the morning, would be worried if she did not get her mother by phone at home. As the patient did not have a cell phone, the social worker obtained a portable phone for her use. Fortunately, the aide brought the patient's pocketbook from home, and the patient had an address book with her important family and friends' numbers. She was able to talk with her daughter, and told her of her fall and being in the Emergency Room, and that the social worker was at her bedside. Her daughter asked to speak with the social worker and expressed her distress about what happened to her mother and her concerns and fears for the future. The social worker was able to put the physician on the phone with the daughter to explain her mother's diagnosis (pending the orthopedic consult) and said that she would in all likelihood require surgery. The social worker gave the daughter information on the hospital's location, where she could park, and how to get to the Emergency Room.

Although the patient had been given some pain medication, she remained very uncomfortable. She was alert, oriented, appeared younger than her stated age, and was responsive to the social worker's interest. She shared that she had been quite independent until recently, and only started to have the services of the aide about a year ago. The aide comes to assist her three days a week.

She had continued to go to the store with the aide to do the shopping, and the aide assisted her with bathing and some food preparation. The aide appeared to treat the patient kindly, and seemed attentive to her needs. The patient was appropriately apprehensive about treatment and the recovery period, having heard from other friends that patients with fractures frequently go to nursing homes.

The orthopedic team came to examine the patient, and confirmed the diagnosis of a fractured hip. They reviewed the patient's medical history, and recommended surgery. The patient was obviously upset and frightened by this information. The social worker encouraged the patient to ask questions of the doctors to allay some of her fears. They reviewed what would be done, and that they found her to be a good surgical candidate, given her functioning prior to the fall, and her lack of other complicating medical issues. She was relieved to hear this, and appeared more at ease.

The social worker received a call from the patient's daughter, who was almost at the hospital, and arranged to meet her in the waiting room. The social worker gave the daughter information as to how her mother appeared, so that she would not be frightened, and accompanied her to the bedside. After the physician provided an explanation of the medical plan for surgery, the social worker described the probable need for rehabilitation following surgery, and some of the options of how and where to get the care her mother would need. She explained that the social worker on the Orthopedic Unit would follow them, and that she would give all the current information to the new worker. They were relieved to hear that the social worker on the orthopedic unit would be there to provide support through this experience, and help them think through the patient's future care needs, transition to the next level of care, and help for the patient to cope emotionally with the implications of aging and the sequelae of this recent physical trauma.

Conclusion

The Emergency Department is also a safe haven for those persons experiencing extreme emotional distress due to issues of depression or other psychological and psychiatric stressors (emotional pain). Social workers have an important role in supporting such patients and assisting them to seek care and in helping to develop a plan for ongoing mental health needs and treatment.

Others requiring assistance from a social worker in the safe haven of the Emergency Department are victims of sexual assault, domestic violence, and child abuse. The social worker helps to sort out issues, defines problems, and works to link patients with the appropriate resources—be they psychological help, financial assistance, housing, or medical treatment.

Carole Friedler is a senior social worker at New York University Medical Center (NYUMC). She is a graduate of Skidmore College and NYU Silver School of Social Work. She has worked at NYUMC since 1975. Ms. Friedler has been the social worker for the emergency room for many years and also worked in critical care, rehabilitation, and cardiovascular surgery.

CHAPTER 14

SOCIAL WORK WITH HOSPITAL PATIENTS

Alma Young, Ed.D., LMSW

Introduction

People are usually admitted to a hospital because a physical ailment, symptom, or accident propelled them to seek specialized or intensive care that is not available in a doctor's office. Some people come to a hospital because they do not have a primary care doctor, or because they have avoided dealing with a symptom until it became a crisis that was too serious to ignore.

In addition to the primary importance of the patient's physical condition or crisis, there are often significant social, emotional, and/or psychological factors that strongly influence how the patient deals with the hospital. In addition to the pain, discomfort, and anxiety of a health crisis, these facts may heighten the tension and stress felt by the patient and his or her family upon admission to the hospital.

In order to address these social and emotional needs, a hospital may utilize the services of a social worker on the hospital's staff to assist the patient and the family to address issues created by the primary disease or medical condition. The special expertise of social workers is to identify and address the impact of the medical situation and the hospitalization on the psychological and emotional functioning of the patient and the family members, taking into account all of the relevant factors – including job loss, children at home, travel time, and financial worries.

The responsibility of a hospital social worker in some hospitals is to evaluate the total situation, including the patient and the family, as well as other people or factors that have an impact on the patient's healing and care. The social worker may alert other health care professionals about the patient's particular personal issues, including family background, culture, language, religion, personality, mental state, or other influences, which may affect the manner in which the patient reacts to the illness, This may be very significant with patients who might otherwise misunderstand, reject, or simply ignore medical information or instructions after discharge from a hospital. It may also be critical in cases where the patient's wishes differ from the family's, or the patient has not revealed critical information to the doctors that may be essential to the diagnosis and treatment.

Case Example: A Young Mother and Her Diabetic Child

Susan, a 25-year-old single parent, brought her 2-year-old son, Al, to the pediatric emergency room with a cold and diaper rash. During the examination she told the doctor that Al had been diagnosed with diabetes at another hospital a month ago. The examining doctor checked this condition and found that Al's blood sugar was unstable (wildly swinging between high and low levels) and realized after talking with Susan that she was not familiar with the disease or how it should be treated.

Diabetes among young children is a chronic illness, generally considered an inherited disease, in which the body cannot metabolize sugar normally. The treatment for this condition may be dietary but in many cases it involves injections of insulin. The goal in treatment is to keep the patient's blood sugar within normal range to avoid complications such as fainting or incoherence.

The social worker talked with Susan about diabetes, specifically what it is, how it affects the body, and the treatments necessary. The immediate plan was to have Al seen in the clinic the next day in order to address these issues more fully and plan a course of treatment for Al and education for his mother.

After considering Al's case, the doctor decided that Al should be admitted to the hospital for further evaluation, stabilization of his insulin doses, and the opportunity for members of the team to spend more time with his mother. Of greatest concern was an assessment of Susan's ability to understand the treatment regimen and to manage it on a daily basis.

The social worker interviewed Susan at Al's bedside. Susan seemed distant and annoyed. Finally, she asked, "What about me? I have no time for myself." This led to a

discussion about family and friends in her life as well as
circumstances leading to her pregnancy and Al's birth. The
social worker discovered that to Susan, the diagnosis of
diabetes felt like another failure in her life and the fact that
it would require so much from her was more than she could
cope with. As the social worker began to focus on Susan's
needs, she became more responsive. Gradually she began
to communicate her needs and the challenges of her
responsibility for her son. As she became more involved in
her son's care, the social worker, along with the other
members of the team and the staff on the floor, laid out a
specific plan for Susan to follow.

As the time for Al's discharge drew closer, it was clear that
Susan's progress regarding management of diabetes was
not where it should be. The hospital social worker
contacted the social worker in charge of the
shelter/residence where Susan and Al lived to arrange for
the Visiting Nurse Service to assist her by providing lessons
on diabetic care. The social worker also set up meetings
with other members of the team and floor staff to discuss
plans for discharge that would ensure Al's safety and
Susan's ongoing education on day-to-day management. The
hospital social worker suggested that she and Susan meet

several times before Al's discharge. During the course of these meetings, Susan talked about her life as a foster child and her loneliness. Eventually she was able to talk about what she learned in the education classes at the hospital as well as her concerns and fears about managing Al's care.

There was evidence that Susan's knowledge of managing the diabetes regimen had improved, as did her interaction with Al. Prior to the discharge, the social worker made sure that all recommendations for management were written for Susan in order to avoid any misunderstanding or confusion. Weekly follow-up appointments to monitor Al's progress and overall health were arranged with the nurse and social worker from the home care agency. The hospital social worker arranged for a part-time homemaker to help relieve some of the stress that Susan was feeling. While there were some setbacks, overall, there was progress in Susan's behavior and her ability to care for Al.

This case example highlights the complexity of situations that are not unusual in emergency rooms around the country. Multiple problems such as poverty, lack of resources, and/or lack of community support, complicate the presenting medical problem. The diagnosis of a chronic illness in a child represents a tremendous threat to the child and the parents, and at times feels like a personal failure to many parents. The initial reaction is usually one of shock, and the parent's resulting emotional turmoil interferes with their ability to hear or understand much of the medical information imparted to them. Generally, the illness affects the coping abilities of the entire family since adjustments must be made to accommodate the child's daily routine as well as his or her medical care. As in this case, the functions of the social worker are not limited to dealing with the patient and with other professionals in the hospital or health care setting. Social workers take responsibility for identifying, communicating with, and arranging collaborations with individuals at other agencies as well.

Even situations with fewer risk factors than the case of Susan and Al may need help from the non-medical staff. An illness can upset the pattern of family life and a family may need a great deal of help in sorting out the impact on them and learning how to cope with a new paradigm.

Case Example: A Social Worker Helps a Family Deal with the Mother's Serious Illness

Katherine, a 41-year-old woman with a husband and two children, aged 12 and 8, was hospitalized after suffering a stroke. She made a good recovery, but had difficulty speaking and was paralyzed on her right side. Although she made progress in regaining strength in therapy, she would need help with personal care at home and would, at least initially, be unable to manage her household. Her husband had a demanding job and was often out of town.

As Katherine's condition stabilized, the social worker met with her and her husband to plan for her discharge. Katherine was very frustrated with her disabilities and often tearful. Her 12-year-old daughter was very helpful at home, but the husband was concerned about the daughter feeling overly responsible. Their 8-year-old son was having trouble in school and was acting out at home. The husband had already hired a housekeeper and his sister was prepared to move into their home for the immediate future to help Katherine and to take care of the children and the family's needs when he was away. The social worker offered to assist in finding a family counselor for the family and a therapist for Katherine. They also discussed the needs of both children and the social worker suggested that the husband ask the school for referrals for counselors for them both. She also suggested that the husband join the hospital's support group for family members who are dealing with sudden medical crises.

The social worker's assistance in this case played a major role in stabilizing the family. Although they had sufficient resources to help each family member cope, and both husband and wife were amenable to counseling, they still needed guidance and recommendations for resources that would meet their daunting new situation.

Conclusion

The complexity of medical illness in some cases requires a multi-disciplinary approach. Social workers are often called in when a family is impoverished and in need of assistance from government agencies. However, even families with resources are often uncertain about how to access counseling or other assistance, or how to tell when family members also need assistance. Having a social worker available on the hospital staff allows the family to obtain the information and assistance necessary for them to move forward as a unit.

Prompt discharges and shortened stays are the reality of hospitals these days. Social workers must deal with family problems within those truncated time frames, even when they believe more time is needed to fully serve the patient. However, the professional obligation to insure a safe discharge is always primary for social workers, who must of necessity deal with decisions of hospital management that they may be able to influence, but cannot control. In the case of Susan and Al, the reality of risk to the child could have supported a longer hospital stay and the team was in a position to advocate for that based on the hospital's interest in risk management. In the end, Al stayed longer than usual due to the social worker's skillful evaluation of the mother's difficulties in understanding or dealing with the reality of Al's diabetes.

In the second case, of Katherine, longer hospitalization was not necessary. The social worker was able to provide guidance and resources in a few quick meetings and phone calls. In each of these cases, the professional social workers had the necessary skills to help the families – an ability to assess the situation quickly and to identify appropriate resources for patient care after discharge.

Dr. Alma T. Young, Ed.D., LMSW (1930- 2012) was a former practitioner, administrator, and educator in the social work department at Mt. Sinai Medical Center. She had a long history of leadership roles both in local and national associations and on boards in organizations providing services to children, adolescents, and families. She taught and wrote in the field of social work as well as in nursing and medicine. She was a board member of the Helen Rehr Center for Social Work Practice.

CHAPTER 15

SOCIAL WORK IN COMMUNITY AGENCIES AND SCHOOLS

Alma Young, Ed.D., LMSW

Introduction

Social workers are available in a wide variety of
community-based agencies to assist children, adults, and
families who are grappling with a range of emotional,
mental, or physical problems. They work in agencies, for
example, that help with child health or behavioral issues,
homelessness, marital problems, and alcoholism and drug
addiction. Some large agencies such as Catholic Charities,
the Jewish Board of Family and Children's Services, the
Federation of Protestant Welfare Agencies, United
Neighborhood Houses, the United Way, and United
Cerebral Palsy also have local offices and affiliates in
various neighborhoods.

Social workers also may be available in public schools, where they offer a variety of services to families in the district such as counseling, play therapy, or tutoring for those with learning disabilities. Some of these services are provided within the school itself; in other cases a child or family may be referred to an appropriate community agency.

Case Example: Assistance to Medically Fragile Children

One particular agency works to insure that medically fragile children are not hospitalized beyond the need for inpatient care and are provided opportunities so that they, and their families, can reach their potential. Services are provided to other family members as needed. The following case is one such example of the holistic approach used by social workers.

Sarah was a single mother of two: Don, age 6, and Betty, age 2. The family lived in a one-room apartment in a motel which serves homeless families. While Betty was the primary client in this case, Don was also in need of special services, and Sarah needed support and direction. At their first meeting at a local agency, the social worker learned that Betty was severely developmentally delayed and had a nasal gastro-tube to assist with her breathing. Don did not attend school regularly. During the interview it became obvious that Sarah was overwhelmed and depressed by her situation, and needed immediate help with medical care for Betty, special attention for Don, and counseling for herself and possibly Don as well. The social worker set up appointments for Betty's medical condition to be evaluated. Arrangements were made for a nurse to visit the home and assess the medical equipment needed to assist with Betty's care. The social worker also contacted Don's teacher to learn more about his irregular attendance and arranged for a homemaker to help Sarah. The home attendant was assigned within a short period, allowing Sarah to take Don to school and to do errands for herself and Betty.

Sarah brought Betty and Don to see a pediatrician who expressed concerns about Betty's seizures and lack of development. Plans were made for Betty to see several medical specialists. In the meantime, a psychiatrist saw Don for evaluation. The social worker also worked with a city housing agency to move the family out of the shelter and into an appropriate apartment. The social worker visited Don's school and talked with his teacher and the guidance counselor about Don's performance and behavior. This was essential in order to get a better understanding of his irregular attendance, which he told his mother was because he didn't like the school. Except for his attendance, the report on Don was good. Usually he was attentive and responded appropriately when called upon. He was appropriately groomed.

The social worker made several home visits during the first six months of contacts with this family in between the medical appointments. Individual sessions and discussions with Sarah revealed conflicts she was having with Betty's father, who did not live in the home, but threatened her at times. The nature of these threats was unclear, but it's likely there was a form of domestic abuse, and there was no doubt that Sarah was afraid, stressed, and overwhelmed by the situation. While some time was devoted to the safety of the family, Sarah's responsibilities for the children and a move to larger living quarters became the primary focus. Eventually, the request for a larger apartment, along with an allowance for furniture, came through.

Shortly thereafter Betty was admitted to the hospital for apnea and diagnosed with cerebral palsy. The agency social worker met with the hospital staff to discuss Betty's needs upon discharge. Arrangements were made for medical equipment, a visiting nurse service, and a home attendant to assist Sarah during the initial stay at home. In the meantime, plans were made for Don to attend camp for a few weeks during the summer. At one of the many home visits, the social worker was encouraged to see Sarah helping Don with homework. Don went to camp and also spent some time with his father during the summer.

Later, Betty was referred to the United Cerebral Palsy Service (UCP) for medical care and other services. She was fitted with braces and a wheelchair. The social worker continued counseling sessions with Sarah to help her do more on her own, such as make phone calls to obtain needed services and other day-to-day activities to facilitate their lives. Once Betty became a regular participant in the UCP Program, her mother became active in parents meetings and was in frequent communication with staff. In addition, she continued to be attentive to Don's needs. The family's case was transferred to UCP for future needs and ongoing counseling.

This case illuminates the way a trained social worker, using a holistic approach, can assist a family with a rather complex array of social, medical, and emotional problems. In this case example Betty's developmental problems exacerbated the already chaotic situation of a single parent, threatened by domestic abuse and living in a homeless shelter. The social worker got to know the family members, diagnosed the problems of each one, and – most significantly -- was extremely hands-on and proactive in providing help. She communicated and collaborated with other service agencies, the government, and medical personnel to accommodate the ill child's ongoing needs and those of the entire family. And just as important, she tapped Sarah's strengths and fostered her ability to use the help offered.

Social Workers in Schools

Schools sometimes offer health and mental health services as important supports for their educational work – particularly those schools that provide special education classes for medically fragile or learning disabled children, or those that have a population of troubled teens. Professional social workers and health care providers staff most of these school-based clinics. These programs are supported by the local board of education and sometimes by foundation grants and other private sources.

The role of the social worker in a school-based program involves assessing potential problems that may interfere with learning, as well as assessing the strengths of the student and the involvement of parents and/or guardians. Typically the social worker gets referrals from teachers, guidance counselors, or other health care providers who may observe behavior problems, sadness, poor attendance, frequent lateness, or other indicators that a student is unhappy.

The social worker's ability to listen, provide helpful information, counsel individually or in groups, and collaborate with other staff and parents or guardians are the critical factors in providing needed support. The social worker also helps the student address his or her inner concerns. Sometimes the social worker may have to pursue a plan with other staff and the family in an effort to accomplish what is best for the student.

Close communication and cooperation from school staff are critical elements for the success of these programs. School-based programs have been credited with improving students' health, increasing their knowledge of contraceptive use, and improving school attendance. In addition to these overall achievements, some students require very special attention during the course of their education.

Case Example: A Complicated Family Crisis

Jane, a 14-year-old student in a special education class for a learning disability and mild emotional problems, was referred to a social worker in the clinic by the crisis intervention teacher when it became known that she was pregnant. Jane and her mother were seen on an emergency basis because the mother, Ms. F, expressed her wish to have Jane terminate the pregnancy. Jane did not agree, and the teacher, who seemed overwhelmed by the situation, indicated a desire to have the social worker make a quick decision for Jane and her mother.

The social worker acknowledged the need for immediate intervention, but she was equally aware of the need for further exploration and discussion before arriving at a conclusion. During the interview Jane was adamant about not having an abortion, saying, "It just doesn't seem right." The social worker learned that the relationship between Jane and the alleged father was non-existent at this point, and that he had denied paternity. While there were times during the interview when Jane seemed ambivalent about her decision to go through with the pregnancy, there was no indication that she was going to comply with her mother's wish. Ms. F remained firm, and eventually told the social worker that she, herself, had an abortion a couple of years ago because she didn't feel that she could assume responsibility for another child. In addition, she felt that given Jane's age, her emotional state, and limited functioning, she was not in a position to take care of a child.

The social worker's concern about Jane's ability to care for a child led to more specific discussion with Jane which made her ambivalence and fear more apparent. Later the social worker took Jane to meet with the nurse clinician for more detailed information about pregnancy, abortion, and child rearing to help her in the process of decision-making. This then led to more information about the boyfriend and especially how the relationship moved from "just friends" to a more intimate one. Jane said "he was nice" and "he made me laugh" a lot.

One day, when they were alone in the house, "it just happened". At this point, Jane was both ashamed and scared. As the interview continued, the social worker suggested an activity Jane could do at home, writing up pro and con index cards to help her in the decision making process.

At the next appointment, the social worker learned that Jane had scheduled an appointment to terminate the pregnancy but failed to keep it. She discussed with Jane her ambivalence and had a session with Jane and her mother to determine next steps. Her mother agreed to arrange a prenatal appointment. At this point, the social worker's focus shifted to making arrangements for Jane to continue in the special education class. Although the norm was for pregnant high school students to attend a special program, the social worker successfully advocated for keeping Jane in her current program, which Jane very much wanted.

This case illustrates the role and functions of the social worker in providing assistance to this young woman. The social worker listened to Jane and to her mother and did not push for an immediate "solution" to this very complicated problem. She made a helpful suggestion for Jane as she tried to come to a decision. She recognized Jane's ambivalence and worked with her and her mother to come to an agreement on next steps. As it became clear that Jane would have the baby, she advocated for her to stay in the special program she needed for her unique situation.

Conclusion

The examples in this chapter of troubled families seeking help from a community agency and a school illuminate the breadth of human problems that professional social workers address, and the distinctive way in which they combine knowledge of human psychology with expertise in identifying and accessing concrete resources to assist clients to solve problems.

Dr. Alma T. Young, Ed.D., LMSW (1930- 2012) was a former practitioner, administrator, and educator in the social work department at Mt. Sinai Medical Center. She had a long history of leadership roles both in local and national associations and on boards in organizations providing services to children, adolescents, and families. She taught and wrote in the field of social work as well as in nursing and medicine. She was a board member of the Helen Rehr Center for Social Work Practice.

CHAPTER 16

SOCIAL WORK WITH HOMELESS FAMILIES AND INDIVIDUALS

Jay Bainbridge, BA, and Susan Nayowith, PhD, LCSW

Introduction

Have you had experience with individuals or families who are homeless?

Have you observed someone sleeping on the street surrounded by all his or her belongings as you walked by? Were you ever approached by someone who asked you for money? Do you know a family who has been threatened with eviction because one of them became ill or lost a job?

This chapter will explain how a social worker can begin to help individuals or families who are homeless.

What Exactly Do We Mean by Homelessness?

Clearly, a person living permanently in a public space or a shelter is homeless. But what if that person had a home, yet refused to go to it? What if he or she lived in substandard housing, or a severely over-crowded apartment? What if he or she had a place that was not permanently available, such as a room with a friend or family member? What if there was not enough room for an entire family to live in one place?

Common practice in the field of homelessness is to distinguish between the "literally homeless" and those "precariously housed." Literal homelessness includes people living in temporary shelters or in places not meant for habitation, such as on the streets, in abandoned buildings, or in transportation hubs. Precariously housed people have a roof over their heads, but the conditions are unsafe and/or temporary or prohibitively expensive and they are at risk of becoming literally homeless.

Who Is Homeless?

For many, the stereotypical image of a homeless person is of an older white male, an alcoholic or substance abuser, possibly with mental illness, living on the streets. In actuality, homeless people are far more diverse. They include families with children (particularly single mothers) as well as men or women living alone.

Shockingly, nearly one quarter of those homeless on any given night are children under age 18. However, families with children are much less likely to be unsheltered than single individuals.

Nearly a quarter of single adult homeless people are chronically homeless, defined as having a disability and either being homeless continuously for a year or more, or having had four episodes in the last three years. There are also homeless adults who are veterans.

Social Workers Working with the Homelessness

There are many causes and symptoms of homelessness. These include mental or physical illness, substance abuse, being the victim of domestic or other violence, loss of work and/or poverty, family disruptions, incarceration, and other shocks. Homelessness is often the final stage in a lifelong series of crises and missed opportunities. Despite the many causes of homelessness, there is one primary solution – namely housing.

Over the past 30 years, the way advocates and public agencies have addressed homelessness has changed. We have learned that though homeless people often have many coincident problems, these need not necessarily be solved in order to maintain housing. In other words, a person does not need to be "housing ready" in order to leave the streets or a shelter.

Many models of service have been developed for individuals to maintain housing despite on-going mental or other health problems, substance abuse, low income, or trauma. In most cases, services are delivered either directly within a supported housing environment, or indirectly through visiting social workers, counselors, and medical staff. In many of these models services are delivered by social workers, volunteers, and advocates.

For example, there are outreach programs for those who live in parks, on the streets, or in squats. Supportive housing meets the financial, social and functional needs of residents. Housing First models work for people moving directly from the street to a home, and have proven to be effective in maintaining housing for those using them, and generally cost effective. Safe Havens (transitional housing facilities for street homeless individuals, which feature more flexible rules and regulations) are for individuals with special needs. Many communities offer Drop-In Centers where individuals can get hot meals, showers, clothing, medical care and employment referrals. Prevention programs help families and individuals avoid the disruption that a move to a shelter can bring. If possible, it is best to prevent homelessness before it happens – by resolving the cases where precariously housed people might lose their current living arrangement.

Case Example: Prevention

A family has lived in their apartment for 8 years. Both parents work and their three children go to school in the neighborhood. The father got injured on the job, could not work, and the family has fallen behind on their rent. The landlord is threatening eviction, and the parents are becoming more and more stressed out. A member of their church referred them to a prevention program for assistance.

The parents met with a prevention social worker at a community-based agency. The social worker referred the family to a legal assistance program to help the father get worker's compensation as well as past and current wages for his injuries. The family also received cash assistance to pay the back rent and other bills until the father received his worker's compensation. In addition, the social worker contacted the landlord who agreed to work with the family and stop the eviction process.

There are many community programs that may prevent homelessness: legal services can help prevent eviction, public benefits can help pay bills, job placement programs can help people find suitable jobs, and financial counseling and money management services can help individuals access short term financial assistance. Social workers will know how to connect their clients with the services and programs that they need.

Case Example: Outreach

A local resident, Mary, is concerned about her 30-year-old nephew, Frank. She contacted a social worker at a community agency and shared her fears.

Frank has had trouble with alcohol and mental health issues for many years. He did not finish college, cannot maintain steady employment, and spends most nights sleeping in a midtown park. Sometimes he asks her for food or money. She does not want him to go hungry, but she also does not want to give him money for alcohol. She is afraid he might not survive another winter outdoors. She cannot allow him to stay in her apartment; he is too disruptive. She cannot afford to pay rent for an apartment for him. She wants him to go to a shelter, but he says he does not like the rules or the other people.

The social worker is part of an outreach team that meets with street homeless individuals. The outreach team found Frank at the park. They told him that his aunt was worried about him. He said he cannot stay in a shelter. The outreach team told Frank that there were other options, such as safe-haven beds, drop-in centers, medical care, and substance abuse services. Frank said he would think about it. The social workers returned each day to speak with Frank. They brought clothing, told him about places that served food, and eventually developed a relationship with him. After a while he trusted them enough to visit the Safe Haven. Eventually, he gave it a try. He also indicated he might try going to AA meetings.

Case Example: Homeless Veterans

Ed served two terms in the Vietnam War. When he returned he married his high school sweetheart, Janet, had three children, and worked as a high school teacher. Sometime after the children grew up and moved out, Janet was diagnosed with cancer. After witnessing her illness and death, Ed could not cope. He stopped working. He eventually lost his home and his car. His children and extended family tried to reason with him, but they were not successful. He met up with some other veterans in a park just outside his town. For the first time in a long time he felt at ease and comfortable within his new community.

Community members did not want to have people sleeping in the park. They contacted a local social service agency that dispatched social workers to meet with the veterans. The veterans were friendly towards the outreach social workers, but rejected the notion of staying in a shelter. They preferred to remain independent and stay on the street.

The social workers came up with a plan to find the veterans a place indoors where they could all go together. They located a suitable facility and discussed the strategy with the veterans and the agency that ran the facility. Ultimately the veterans agreed to move. The social workers who were located at the facility assisted the veterans with public benefits, substance abuse issues, and housing options.

Many communities have specific services for veterans, such as housing, medical care, local and federal entitlements (pension and public assistance). With the help of the social workers veterans can apply for rental assistance, vouchers and case management services.

Case Example: Shelter Services

Lydia and her two young children came to a family intake center for the homeless after her extended family was evicted from the apartment they shared. Her mother and stepfather went to stay with an aunt, but there was no room for anyone else. Lydia, a woman in her early 20's, had been a stay at home mom. She did not work or collect any public benefits. Her parents took care of her, although they resented the fact that she did not hold a job. Lydia said she could not work since she had young children. Reluctant to ask for help, Lydia did eventually give permission for the social worker to contact her mother.

Lydia agreed to participate in a training program or get employment, while her parents helped watch her children. She and her children were able to stay with the family. Lydia's family ultimately returned to the aunt's house and benefitted from services provided by a community-based organization.

Conclusion

Homelessness is a multi-faceted issue and the social worker must assess the particular needs of each client. As in all of the work they do, the social worker starts where the clients are. Did the client come for help voluntarily or involuntarily? Did they come to the agency and seek assistance or did they come looking for concrete assistance and the social worker was a part of the package? What if anything, do they say they want? Homelessness is more than a need for shelter. People who are homeless need counseling, resources, and assistance with accessing resources, health care, mental health counseling and support.

Jay Bainbridge, BA, Marist College School of Management, is a former Assistant Commissioner for Policy and Planning at the New York City Department of Homeless Services.

Susan Nayowith, PhD., LCSW is adjunct faculty at Hunter College School of Social Work.

CHAPTER 17

SOCIAL WORK IN LEGAL SERVICES AGENCIES

Laurel W. Eisner, JD, MSW

Introduction

Many agencies that provide legal services hire social workers to assist the attorneys to provide effective representation and related services to their clients. These lawyer-social work teams are particularly effective in cases involving allegations of child neglect or abuse, domestic violence, elder abuse, juvenile delinquency and prostitution, or conflicts over child custody. While the lawyer analyzes the client's legal case and represents the client in court proceedings, the social worker provides essential ancillary services that can enhance the client's chances of a successful legal outcome. The social worker may, for example, do a psychosocial evaluation of the client and the family, provide short term counseling and/or crisis intervention, assist the client to access concrete services such as housing, public benefits, medical care, or drug treatment, or advocate for the client in meetings and appointments with government agencies.

Social workers may also be retained by an attorney who has been appointed by the court as a law guardian for a minor in a divorce or custody proceeding. The law guardian's role is to represent the child's interests and wishes, and a social worker or psychiatrist may be appointed by the court, or retained by the law guardian, to evaluate the child and assist in the determination of the child's concerns, problems, and wishes. Some large legal services organizations have social workers on staff to perform such evaluations for the law guardians.[7] In agencies providing services to immigrants, social workers may be asked to do an in depth psycho-social interview with the client to gather

[7]A social worker who works directly with, and is supervised by, an attorney is deemed to be an "agent" of the attorney and is thus protected by a very strict form of confidentiality known as "attorney-client privilege." This privilege bars disclosure to any third party of the attorney's/social worker's records and conversations with the client. In social services settings where the attorneys and social workers collaborate, but the attorney does not supervise the social worker, her/his records do not have the benefit of this strong statutory privilege, and a court may order the records to be disclosed in order to protect the "best interests of the child".

complex background information that may facilitate – or interfere with - - the client's likelihood of obtaining a particular immigration law remedy, such as asylum. In agencies serving victims of domestic violence, the social worker may provide individual or group counseling to assist the client to gain an understanding of the dynamics of domestic abuse and to overcome her profound feelings of guilt and loss of self-esteem as a result of the years of humiliating psychological abuse at the hands of the abuser. With this increased understanding, the client may be a better advocate for herself – with the batterer and in court proceeding regarding divorce, custody or visitation.

Case Example: Lawyer-Social Work Teams Assisting Parents Accused of Abuse

Ms. H is a single mother who was accused by the city's child protective services agency (CPS) of using excessive corporal punishment with her 11 year old son. CPS sought permission from the Family Court to remove both of Ms. H's children from her home. The court assigned a lawyer from a legal services agency that specialized in family law ("the agency") to represent Ms. H. The court ordered removal of the children pending trial on the complaint against Ms. H. and both children were placed in foster care. Ms. H. was granted limited supervised visits with them.

The agency attorney and social worker team interviewed Ms. H and learned that she had no prior history of accusations of abuse; they also found many inconsistencies in CPS's version of the alleged event. The social worker accompanied Ms. H to service planning conferences, which are convened by CPS to develop a service plan for the families who are subject to CPS' jurisdiction. Social workers are permitted to attend these conferences with the clients, although attorneys are prohibited from doing so.

The social worker prepared Ms. H for the conference explaining who would be there and how the conference would proceed. They discussed the allegations against Ms. H and what services the client felt would benefit her. She advised Ms. H that CPS would probably ask her to take a drug test, even thought she had no prior history of substance abuse. The social worker explored the client's history and assessed the likelihood of substance abuse. The worker also assessed Ms. H's understanding of the severity of the situation, the importance of being truthful in the conference, and the consequences of any agreements or commitment she would make during the conference.

During this discussion, the client was able to articulate some of the tensions that her family was facing such as the loss of the children's father the previous year, her lack of financial stability, her poor relationships with her own family and the lack of personal supports when she most needed them.

The social worker suggested that Ms. H consider sharing some of these problems at the conference and asking for help -- perhaps family counseling, financial assistance with a housing subsidy, and bereavement counseling for her sons if they were willing to go. They discussed a plan in which the client would be open to these supportive services but would reject any substance abuse testing. They even discussed which one of them – the client or the social worker – would speak up if these were suggested. The client wanted the social worker to do so and felt she was already very vulnerable by sharing these deep struggles with a group of people who may judge her or decide when her sons could come home.

At the meeting, the social worker sat with the client and introduced herself as the client's advocate. CPS initially recommended sending Ms. H to multiple services in different neighborhoods, including a substance abuse treatment program, despite the absence of evidence of substance abuse by Ms. H. The social worker advocated for a better plan, and assisted in referring Ms. H to one agency that could provide multiple services on site. The social worker and lawyer reported regularly to the CPS on Ms. H's progress in the prescribed services and CPS soon modified the terms of Ms. H's visits with the children from supervised to unsupervised visitation. When the Family court case on the allegation of excessive corporal punishment finally came to trial, the Judge dismissed the neglect case against Ms. H and the family was reunified immediately after the children had spent four months in foster care.

Case Example: Lawyer-Social Work Teams Assisting Parents Accused of Neglect

Ms. S was a young mother accused by the Child Protective Services agency (CPS) of child neglect by failing to protect them from witnessing domestic violence in the home, and by using marijuana. A relative of Ms. S apparently had made these and other allegations against Ms. S in a series of anonymous calls to the State Central Registry of Child Abuse and Neglect. CPS sought to place Ms. S's children in foster care.

A lawyer assigned by the court to represent Ms. S, working with a social worker, explored Ms. S's history and discovered that all of the prior complaints to the Central Registry had been investigated and then dismissed as "unsubstantiated". The team presented that information to the judge on Ms. S's case, along with convincing evidence that Ms. S did not use drugs. As a result of this advocacy, the Judge adjourned Ms. S's case with the understanding that CPS's complaint would be dismissed if Ms. S had no further problems within the next six months.

Unfortunately, the anonymous complainant continued to report baseless allegations to the Central Registry, including an allegation of medical neglect of Ms. S's 4 year old son the prior year. Instead of doing a full investigation into the medical neglect allegation, Child Protective Services asked the court to order an emergency removal of the children from Ms. S's home. Citing concerns about her history, the court placed her 4-year old and 9-month old children in foster care.

The same lawyer-social work team was re-assigned to this family. Based on their earlier work and some additional investigation, the team assessed that the allegations were baseless. They immediately petitioned for another emergency court hearing, this time to urge that the children be returned to Ms. S's care. During the hearing, the judge and the CPS representative expressed their concerns about the earlier allegations of domestic violence. Child Protective Services had a long past history of considering a victim of domestic violence responsible for the detrimental impact of the violence on the children if she failed to keep the batterer out of the home. Failing to take appropriate and reasonable steps to do so could be considered child neglect under the state law.

As the hearing proceeded, the social worker provided the court with detailed, up to date information about the social work counseling Ms. S had received, and how the counseling and related services had enabled Ms. S to gain insight into the dynamics of domestic violence and thus terminate the abusive relationship. The social worker also testified that Ms. S had become more mature through these services and her parenting skills had improved considerably. After the hearing, the Judge reversed the order of emergency removal of the children and returned them to Ms. S's care. The judge scheduled a future hearing where the various allegations of neglect would be reviewed, with the lawyer-social work team again representing Ms. S In the meantime, Ms. S's children were back home with her and she was able to continue to receive counseling and other social work assistance from the social worker on her case.

Conclusion

These are fairly typical case studies of child welfare cases. They highlight the essential role the social workers play in fulfilling the agency's mandate to ensure that a parent accused of neglect of abuse has a full and fair opportunity to address, and/or challenge, the allegations against her. With a social worker's special training and expertise, she can develop a relationship with the client and gather personal, family and social-psychological background information relevant to the case. The social worker is then in a position to provide a balanced picture of the client and the family to the attorney on the team, and, where appropriate, to the court and the CPS investigators.

The social worker may also actively assist the client with concrete problems that are barriers to return of the children, such as inappropriate or dangerous housing, of the lack of essential government benefits.

In cases where the court does not accept the client's petition for return of her children, the social worker can continue to assist the client to meet the CPS requirements and to assist the parent to make decisions about how to go forward – with mental health counseling, psychiatric assistance, parenting classes, or other support services to facilitate speedy reunification with her children. While reunification is not always the outcome in CPS cases, absent clear evidence of grave and imminent harm to the children, it is always the desired result given the cost and the known social hazards of foster care.

Laurel W. Eisner, JD, MSW, teaches organizational management, leadership and non-profit governance at the

Silberman School of Social Work, and provides consulting services in those areas. From 2002-2013, she was the Executive Director of Sanctuary for Families, an agency providing victims of domestic violence and sex trafficking with clinical, legal services and shelter services. Before that she was the General Counsel for the New York City Public Advocate, Mark Green, and an Assistant Attorney General of the State of New York.

CHAPTER 18

A SOCIAL WORKER CAN HELP YOU FIND THE SERVICES YOU NEED

Penny Schwartz, DSW, LCSW

Introduction

There is a vast array of government and private entitlements and benefits programs, which can be helpful to people with a range of psychological, social, and economic needs. Even the most informed person can have trouble knowing what services are available and how to access and utilize them. Complicating this process is the fact that the criteria for obtaining and maintaining these benefits frequently changes as federal, state, and local laws are amended or new laws implemented.

Social workers are uniquely trained to provide information, advocacy, and assistance with the application process, eligibility requirements, and utilization of these programs. By availing oneself of social work services, clients can gain a clearer understanding of what may be helpful to them and their families when trying to cope with the impact of illness on their lives.

Social workers can perform a "differential entitlement assessment" in which they compile the facts of a client's situation, consider how the clients' needs might be best addressed by the available services, and then share that evaluation with the client. A patient or family who had to obtain all this information on their own might well get incomplete or inaccurate information because they are not familiar with the various systems and services in the community. The social worker can help decide which services might be most beneficial to the client and family and then assist them with the often daunting process of obtaining and maintaining the benefit.

Case Example: Benefits for a Severely Ill Father

A social work intervention assisted a family of four in which the father was severely asthmatic and could not work outdoors, which impacted his ability to hold his job. The physician's letter and medical records did not stop the public assistance office from closing their case and withholding Medicaid assistance. The gentleman was left without his asthma medication and the children did not have access to their routine medical care. This resulted in a severe asthma attack that required hospitalization. Prior to his discharge, the social worker intervened with the public assistance office, and got his benefits restored retroactive to the date of the erroneous sanction.

Case Example: Public Assistance Withdrawn

A 37-year-old mother of three could not attend a work assessment interview because she had an emergency appointment at school concerning her emotionally disturbed son. Although the principal of the school contacted the work program to explain the mother's situation, the public assistance office discontinued all cash,

*medical, and food assistance benefits for 45 days. The
social worker advocated for this family by "going up the
chain" until she reached the welfare center director, who
acknowledged the error and restored their benefits
retroactive to the date of application.*

Case Example: Helping a Family

*This case involved a 7-month pregnant mother, her
husband who had just been diagnosed with a late-stage
testicular cancer, and their two-year-old daughter. The
husband initially had insurance through his job, which
terminated shortly after his diagnosis and initial surgery.
The family received a notice that the landlord was going to
start eviction proceedings. Because the patient was going
to have to undergo a bone marrow transplant and other
therapies, he could not return to work and was expected to
be disabled for an undetermined period of time. This young
family had no way to pay their rent, buy food, or obtain
medical coverage. Additionally, the husband could not be
placed on the transplant list until his ability to pay for post-
transplant medications and follow-up care had been
established. For several months prior to and for several*

weeks after her husband's diagnosis this mother tried to apply for cash, medical and food assistance. The patient has an emergent admission and the hospital social worker assessed that they had a "high-risk" situation. She intervened with both the Medicaid and public assistance programs to get all the benefits to which this family was entitled. The husband received his life saving medical care, the mother got the appropriate pre-natal care and delivered a healthy baby, and their young daughter got all her "well child" care.

Conclusion

These examples are but a few of the ways in which social work intervention has been necessary to help people get and maintain the care they need. By assisting people with obtaining their entitlement benefits social workers help lessen the potentially negative impact that illness and hospitalization can have on the patient and the family.

Dr. Penny Jeffra Schwartz received her Doctor of Social Welfare from Hunter College School of Social Work and her Masters of Science in Social Work from Columbia University School of Social Work. She has served as an Adjunct Professor at both the Hunter College School of Social Work and Fordham University Graduate School of Social Science. In 2004 she was elected as a Fellow of the New York Academy of Medicine. Dr. Schwartz was a program coordinator at The Mount Sinai Medical Center where she founded the Resource Entitlement Advocacy Program. She was awarded the Distinguished Service Award in 2003 and again in 2014 for her advocacy efforts on behalf of the elderly, disabled and poor by the Sadin Institute on Law of the Brookdale Center on Healthy Aging and Longevity of Hunter College.

CONCLUSION: FINDING REAL SOLUTIONS

This book demonstrates how social workers are helpful in a variety of situations. If you need the services and the help of a social worker, you can contact the local offices of a religious organization, such as Catholic Charities, the Federation of Protestant Welfare Agencies, the Federation of Jewish Agencies (UJA), or a local mosque, to name a few. Such organizations typically provide services based on need, not based on religion.

Local community service agencies, which provide services for children, adolescents, adults, or the elderly, can also help directly or provide referrals.

Hospitals typically have social workers that provide inpatient services and they sometimes also provide outpatient services for the local community.

Civic groups, such as the Chamber of Commerce or Kiwanis, may refer those in need to local service agencies. Community churches and schools can also make referrals.

If you need the help of a social worker, any of these resources will be able to assist you.